BUYING DISNEY'S WORLD

BUYING DISNEY'S WORLD

THE STORY OF HOW FLORIDA SWAMPLAND BECAME WALT DISNEY WORLD

AARON H. GOLDBERG

Quaker Scribe Publishing

Buying Disney's World
Copyright © 2021 by Aaron H. Goldberg
All rights reserved.

Cover design by Rob Yeo Design
Interior layout and typesetting by Sue Balcer

Published by Quaker Scribe Publishing
Philadelphia, Pennsylvania
quakerscribe@gmail.com

First printing 2021
Paperback ISBN: 978-1-7336420-5-7
Hardcover ISBN: 978-1-7336420-6-4
Library of Congress Control Number: 2020924501

Visit the author on the web: www.aaronhgoldberg.com
Follow Aaron H. Goldberg on Twitter & Instagram at @aaronhgoldberg

For my late mother, Susan,
who always encouraged me to dream big

CONTENTS

INTRODUCTION

To the cast, on the eve of Walt Disney World's opening day, may I thank all of you for your spirt—your cooperation and the fine job all of you have done in getting ready for our opening. Years of planning and long hours of work have brought about this historic moment. It will be an experience none of us will forget. At this time I think it is appropriate that we remember Walt's comment: 'You can dream, design and build the most wonderful place in the world but it requires people to make the dream a reality.' You, the cast, are responsible for making Walt's dream come true . . . yesterday, today and tomorrow. [1]

—Roy O. Disney, Chairman of The Board

On the evening before Walt Disney World opened, Roy O. Disney's words above, along with the words from his younger brother, Walt, illustrated the Disney brothers' appreciation and recognition for their employees during their company's grandest and most challenging project to date.

Although, at times the brothers were difficult to work for. Walt was perhaps more of an ardent task master than Roy, but both men expected a tremendous amount from their employees—and from themselves.

Brothers first and business partners second—or maybe at times it was the other way around—the two men often squabbled with each other and had a few legendary fights that strung on for months at a time.

Ultimately, they always resolved their differences and came together to innovate and shape the world of entertainment.

Walt and Roy were geniuses in their respective fields: Walt, a legendary dreamer, entertainment industry maven, and pop culture influencer—decades before the concept even existed—and Roy, a fiscal and financial mastermind, uncomfortable in the spotlight but certainly comfortable with the bank ledger (as you will read later, Roy opened the gates to Walt Disney World basically debt free).

Buying Disney's World is the story of the brothers' last project together, which culminated in the creation of Walt Disney World.

On the surface, this book tells the interesting and detailed story of how Walt Disney World came to be—which at times reads like a spy novel.

However, just below the surface, there's a peripheral story of how one man's dream evolved into another man's dream—most likely a scenario neither man envisioned at the onset of the project.

Walt was always the driving force behind his and his brother's projects, while Roy, creatively speaking, was often just along for the ride. As Roy reflected in 1970:

We were novices and operating on a shoestring. We really did not know what we were doing. He did the dreaming. I did the building.

We learned with Disneyland. That was the start of this idea Walt had. As we went along, he got other ideas, and I guess I really never doubted that we would someday be here at Walt Disney World.

That is, I may not have known where it would be located and there were lots of times I wasn't even certain of what it would be, and told Walt so, but I figured that someday something would happen, and so a few years after opening Disneyland we began formulating and financing some of Walt's ideas, and so here we are.[2]

When the Disney brothers began acquiring land in central Florida, Walt was in his sixties and Roy was in his seventies. A little more than a year after the Disney World project was announced to the public, Walt passed away, on December 15, 1966—he was sixty-five years old.

With Walt gone, Roy took over his brother's final dream. He put off his retirement and oversaw the project, ensuring that at least part of Walt's vision for the land they purchased in Florida came to fruition.

At the peak of construction, in 1970, the Vacation Kingdom, as it was then called, was the largest private construction project in the United States.

With more than 10,000 workers on site—representing just about every type of building and construction trade—nearly ten million cubic yards of earth were moved to create the necessary infrastructure for a theme park and two cities.

The workers then curated, sculpted, and transformed what was, just a few short years earlier, 27,443 acres—the property runs twelve miles long and seven miles wide[3]—of swamps, orange groves, and cow pastures into the world's most visited theme park and resort.

The construction stories and technological advancements featured at Walt Disney World when it debuted are quite interesting, and we will get to many of them toward the end of the book.

However, the story we are really interested in isn't about the thousands of people who helped shape Disney's land in central Florida. It's about the handful of people who acquired the acreage for Disney and the covert process they went through to obtain it.

The key players involved in this top-secret mission were well connected in the business world and in the world of espionage.

An integral member of Disney's land-acquisition team was a high-ranking CIA operative who, just a few short years prior, was rumored to be the paymaster behind the Bay of Pigs Invasion in Cuba.

This savvy and influential CIA agent became the de facto leader for the group of Disney executives and attorneys who orchestrated and executed a nearly perfect plan to keep Disney's identity a secret from the public.

Staying true to Disney's storytelling roots, these men wove a tale of mystery with aliases, shell corporations, and meandering travel itineraries in an effort to scoop up thousands of acres without disclosing who was buying the property and what it was going to be used for.

Once their clandestine land acquisition was complete, the project was far from over. There was more wrangling and finagling to do.

This powerful group of advisors and attorneys implored the Disney company to create its own municipality, not bound by statues and ordinances at the state or county level. The new kingdom should be completely controlled by Disney—a publicly traded company—which, at the time, was most famously known for creating Mickey Mouse.

Could the state of Florida allow Disney to wield nearly absolute legal control over its property under a quasi-government municipality? As we already know, the answer is yes.

But how did all of this happen? How did Disney carve out its own fiefdom in central Florida?

By utilizing the personal notes and files from the key figures involved in the project, *Buying Disney's World* answers these questions and tells the entire story of how Walt Disney World came to be, like you've never heard before.

Buying Disney's World goes from the inception of the project, to the land purchases, to the creation of Disney's municipality (the Reedy Creek Improvement District), and finally, to the construction of Walt Disney World—and everything in between.

Before we dive into the story, I must thank the folks at the Reedy Creek Improvement District for answering my questions and providing me with detailed and crucial information about the District.

Another big thank you goes to the University of Central Florida Library's Special Collections Archives for allowing me to access two of their collections.

The first is the Harrison "Buzz" Price collection. Price was a research economist who helped Walt Disney hand pick the locations for Disneyland and Walt Disney World.

The second is the Disney World Land Purchase/RCID Collection, compiled by attorney Robert P. Foster. Foster headed up the land acquisition for Walt Disney World.

Being able to study the documents from the men directly involved in the creation of Walt Disney World was invaluable. At times it almost made me feel as though I was sitting in on the top secret meetings with Walt and Roy decades ago.

Hopefully I can convey a glimmer of this feeling to you as well.

—Aaron H. Goldberg, December 2020

THE GOLDEN TOUCH

By 1966 the world's population came in at 3.395 billion. The United States made up 196.6 million of that total.[1]

Here are a few other numbers for you from 1966: 240 million people saw a Disney movie that year; 100 million people a week watched a Disney television show; 80 million read a Disney book; 50 million listened to a Disney record; 150 million read a Disney comic strip; and 7 million visited Disneyland.[2]

These were (and still are) pretty remarkable numbers. Yet despite this incredible amount of success, according to Walt Disney, his biggest and grandest project was just beginning to come together down in central Florida.

Walt was no stranger to the Sunshine State. In fact, the Disney family's ties to central Florida stretch back further and run deeper than a theme park on some swampland near a sleepy town called Orlando.

In the late 1880s, a man by the name of Elias Disney settled in the town of Acron, in Lake County, Florida, about an hour north of Orlando. (Today, Acron is a ghost town and has been swallowed up by the Ocala National Forest.)

A young woman by the name of Flora Call also lived in the town, along with her family, on an orange farm. Flora was trained as a schoolteacher, and she had been the second teacher hired in Acron.

During the late 1880s, Acron had a population of about 300 residents. So, it wouldn't take much for Elias—who was delivering mail by horse in town—to encounter and become smitten with a young schoolmistress named Flora.

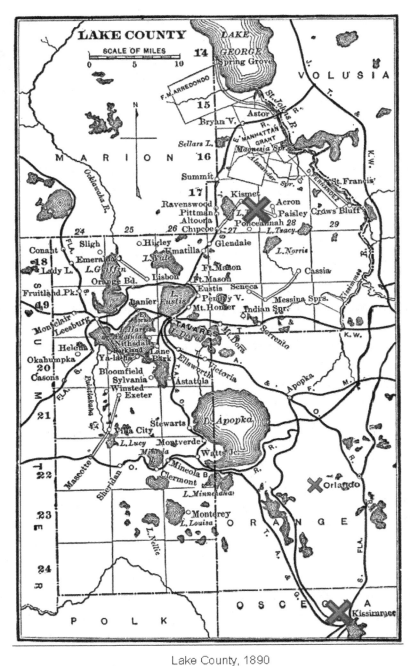

Lake County, 1890

After a short courting period, nearly thirty-year-old Elias and nearly twenty-year-old Flora were married on New Year's Day in 1888. Their union was the first licensed marriage in Lake County, Florida.

Now a married man looking to put down roots in the area, Elias gave up his postal route and tried his hand as an orange farmer. This occupation was short lived, as a deep freeze destroyed most of his crop.

Looking for a new opportunity away from farming, Elias decided to move his family to Chicago in 1890. A year prior, Elias's brother Robert had relocated there to capitalize on the blossoming business and employment opportunities due to the upcoming Chicago World's Fair of 1893 (also known as the World's Columbian Exposition).

Elias found work as a carpenter in Chicago, and over the next thirteen years, he fathered four children: Raymond, Roy, Walt, and Ruth. The eldest Disney child, Herbert, had been born in Florida before the family relocated.

Courtesy of Lake County, Florida

While the Disney family moved on from central Florida rather quickly, the Call family stayed in the area for decades.

As Walt and Roy grew older, they periodically visited the maternal side of their family in Florida, most notably their Great Aunt Jessie. (If you're looking for a quick side trip while visiting Walt Disney World, take a drive about fifty miles north to Ponceannah Cemetery, off of County Road 42, and pay homage to Walt and Roy's maternal grandparents, Charles and Henrietta Call.)

Great Aunt Jessie even made a trip out to Hollywood to visit her famous nephews in the 1950s. When she got back to Florida, she gave her friends the lowdown on Walt and Roy: "Those two boys are borrowing an excessive amount of money for some kind of fool circus thing. They really know how to spend money."[3]

Aunt Jessie wasn't the only person who thought Walt's new project, Disneyland, was a fool circus—most people did, even his brother Roy.

Walt Disney visiting with Aunt Jessie Perkins and cousin, Irene Campbell in

Courtesy of the Florida Memory Project

The idea of Disneyland, and how that all came to be, is a book unto itself, and it has been chronicled countless times in countless books by countless authors, myself included. Therefore, I won't go into too much detail about its creation. I'll leave it up to Walt to briefly tell us where Disneyland came from:

Disneyland really began when my two daughters were very
young. Saturday was always Daddy's day, and I would take

them to the merry-go-round, and sit on a bench eating peanuts, while they rode. And sitting there, alone, I felt there should be something built, some kind of family park where parents and children could have fun together.

I'd be sitting there trying to figure out what I could do. It took many years. I started with many ideas, threw them away, and started all over again. And eventually it evolved into what you see today at Disneyland.[4]

What we see today at Disneyland is more than just a place for family fun—it's a game changer. Disneyland was a catalyst for the family entertainment genre, and it left an indelible mark on culture around the world.

It appears as though Aunt Jessie was wrong about Walt's whole "fool circus" thing. However, she was right about one thing: Walt *really* did know how to spend money. He once recounted:

I had different cost estimates; one time it was three and a half million and then I kept fooling around a little more with it and it got up to seven and a half million and I kept fooling around a little more and pretty soon it was twelve and a half and I think when we opened Disneyland it was seventeen million dollars.[5]

As Walt said, Disneyland opened in July of 1955 at a cost of over $17 million dollars. He had to practically beg, borrow, and steal to get the funding he needed to open up his Magic Kingdom.

In the end, it was all worth it. The world loved Walt's theme park. Two years after Disneyland opened, *Time* magazine took note and had this to say: "Thanks to Disney's pixelating power to strike the youthful nerve of Americans, Disneyland is proving to be America's biggest tourist attraction."[6]

Disneyland elevated and redefined the theme park genre. People visited in droves, and they continued to do so today. As a result, a permanent mark has been left on the park's hometown, Anaheim.

As Walt once joked after Disneyland opened:

Anaheim was a town of 14,000 then, and if someone had mentioned that one year soon six million visitors would come to Disneyland, folks might have had second thoughts about inviting us. In fact, we might have had second thoughts about building a Disneyland![7]

What was once a rural farming community quickly became a cluster of restaurants, liquor stores, motels, and retail shops. At the epicenter of this explosive growth was Disneyland.

Walt didn't fully expect this aftershock of consumerism on his doorstep. An entire cottage industry popped up outside of Disneyland, and Walt disliked every iota of it:

One of the things I've learned from Disneyland is to control the environment. Without that we get blamed for the things that someone else does. When they come here, they're coming because of integrity that we've established over the years, and they drive for hundreds of miles and the little hotels on the fringe jump their rates three times. I've seen it happen and I just can't take it because, I mean, it reflects on us. I just feel a responsibility to the public when I go into this thing that we must control that, and when they come into this so-called world, that we will take the blame for what goes on.[8]

A second-rate Las Vegas, as he often called it, encroached on his Magic Kingdom. It ruined the allure and illusion of what he had worked so hard to create. As he once said: "I don't want the public to see the world they live in while they're in Disneyland. I want them to feel they're in another world."[9]

Walt loved his Disneyland, but he despised what surrounded it. He couldn't shake the feeling that the real world tainted his fantasy world. If he had the opportunity to do it all over again, would he? Perhaps a better question was, should he?

Chapter 2

LIVING WITH THE LAND

From mid-July 1955 to 1958, over ten million people visited Disneyland. Two-thirds of the park's visitors came from California, and only 8 percent came from east of the Mississippi.[1]

Disneyland received an enormous amount of media attention. Combined with a television show of the same name dominating TV markets nationwide, it began taking shape as a regional theme park and cultural landmark. The former didn't necessarily thrill Walt.

In many respects, Disneyland is a victim of its own success. Due to financial constraints, Walt wasn't able to buy enough land around the park to keep other businesses at bay—a subject Walt frequently brought up to those around him.

Another dilemma stemming from not having a huge swath of land was an issue with future expansion and capacity concerns. Over the decades, the park has expanded and grown. As it has grown, demand has grown; even today, capacity issues plague Disneyland.

There really wasn't much Walt could do to remedy these situations. After Disneyland opened, adjacent real estate prices soared, and the infiltration around his park had already commenced.

With an almost inescapable eye for perfection, and an obsessive personality when it came to his creative worlds, a few quotes from Walt should give you a glimpse into how he processed the state of affairs both inside and outside of Disneyland—along with how he believed he could resolve it:

> *"By nature I'm an experimenter. To this day, I don't believe in sequels. I can't follow popular cycles. I have to move on to new things."*[2]

"I happen to be kind of an inquisitive guy and when I start to see things I don't like, I start thinking, why do they have to be like this and how can I improve them?"[3]

"I see only mistakes we made. It's like going over a theme you wrote in grade school."[4]

"A picture is a thing that once you wrap it up and turn it over to Technicolor, you're through. Snow White is a dead issue with me. The last picture I just finished—the one I just wrapped up a few weeks ago—it's gone; I can't touch it. There's things in it I don't like. I can't do anything about it."[5]

"I wanted something live, something that could grow, something I could keep plussing with ideas, you see? The park is that. Not only can I add things but even the trees will keep growing; the thing will get more beautiful every year. And as I find what the public likes—and when a picture's finished and I put it out—I find out what they like, or they don't like, and I have to apply that to some other thing; I can't change that picture, so that's why I wanted that park."[6]

"Ideas come from curiosity. When I settle one idea, my confidence takes command; nothing can shake it, and I am constant to it until it comes a reality."[7]

"I can never stand still. I must explore and experiment. I am never satisfied with my work. I resent the limitations of my own imagination."[8]

Walt loved his Disneyland; it was his muse, in a sense. He would continue to "plus it" and grow it as best he could. But after the first few years, he couldn't ignore the glaring limitations and the mistakes.

As quoted, he wasn't a believer in sequels. Walt *was* a huge believer in progress, though. Disneyland was progress on so many levels, despite the shortcomings perhaps only he perceived.

Walt wanted, and needed, another opportunity to right his theme park wrongs. Conceivably, another project on a larger piece of land could provide him with the buffer he needed from the outside world.

This would also enable him to create something where visitors could lengthen the duration of their stay to days, instead of the mere hours typically spent at Disneyland.

His new project wouldn't exactly be a sequel, but Disneyland could be used as a schematic, as it revealed to him what worked, didn't work, and could work.

By 1958, just three years after Disneyland opened, the notion of creating something else was looming large inside Walt's brain. But where should the project go? He thought, perhaps, he would have to go east, go big, and stay in control of everything. However, he needed more research to confirm his thoughts.

That year he commissioned research economist Buzz Price—who helped Walt pinpoint the location for Disneyland—to determine if his feelings were correct, and if indeed, the East Coast could be primed for Disneyland East, or something like it.

In the meantime, since Disneyland had opened, opportunity had constantly been knocking on Walt's door. Businessmen from around the world started courting him in hopes of having him replicate his theme park, often offering the land or funding for the project for free.

One such enticing business plan came from a group composed of the RCA Corporation, NBC, and John D. MacArthur, the head of Banker's Life Insurance. MacArthur owned thousands of acres near West Palm Beach (a portion of this land is now used by the Professional Golf Association).

The group wanted to create a planned community on MacArthur's land called the City of Tomorrow, featuring a theme park and an art school. The Disney brothers weren't in love with the situation; they were afraid they wouldn't have enough control over the project, so they passed.[9]

Roy did have a memorable trip on a site visit to the property, though. He got a huge kick out of MacArthur's chauffeured limo, which had hydraulic lifters so the vehicle could be raised to drive over the rough terrain of the land. When Roy got back to Southern California, it's all he could talk about, which showed how he felt about the actual proposed project.[10]

Another proposition that was shelved was Riverfront Square in St. Louis. This project actually received a name and a set of blueprints. The idea was to revitalize downtown St. Louis with an enclosed Disney attraction. Ultimately, finances, control, and ownership did this project in.

At the time, some folks concluded that August Busch Jr., from the legendary beer brewing family, hadn't helped the cause when he commented that Walt Disney was crazy to think a project without alcohol could succeed in Busch's town.

There was one project that did catch Walt's eye: a bowling alley— yes, you're reading that correctly.

Back in the late 1950s and 1960s, the sport of bowling took the United States by storm. The Professional Bowlers Association (PBA) was formed in 1958. A few short years later, the PBA tour was televised nationally on ABC Sports and had major sponsors such as Coca-Cola and Ford Motor Company.[11]

By 1963, Harry Smith, the country's top bowler, made more money than Major League Baseball's MVP, Sandy Koufax, and the NFL's MVP, Y. A. Tittle, combined.[12]

During the early 1960s, 12,000 new bowling alleys opened for business in the US. One of those new alleys was opened near Denver, Colorado by a group of Hollywood celebrities led by none other than Walt Disney.

As comedic legend Jack Benny said at the time: "Here's the situation. Several years ago, Walt Disney caught a mouse. He parlayed that into a fortune. Now, if he can do that, do you think I'm going to miss an opportunity like this to turn a buck?"[13]

Clearly, Jack Benny was on board to open the alley with Walt, as was George Burns and Gracie Allen, Burl Ives, Bing Crosby, Charles Laughton, Spike Jones, Art Linkletter, and John Payne.

Even the extended Disney family got involved. Walt's daughter Diane and her husband Ron joined Walt, and Roy and Roy's son, Roy E. Disney, along with his wife, rounded out the investment group.

In September of 1960, the $6 million-dollar Celebrity Sports Center opened for business—a fitting name with that ownership group.

The facility had eighty bowling lanes, seating for five hundred, a billiard room, a game room, a restaurant and lounge, a Hofbrau room featuring beer and sandwiches, a pro shop, and a barber shop.

Walt Disney and Art Linkletter, famous Radio & T.V. showmen, were both enthusiastic sports fans, and both dedicated to developing family entertainment and family recreation.

They had worked closely together in many ventures, including the staging of pageantry for the 1960 Winter Olympics at Squaw Valley for which Walt Disney was pageant chairman. Both were mountain lovers and ski enthusiasts. They thought that Denver was an ideal place to develop what was at that time a new dimension in family recreation.

They interested other Hollywood personalities, also pictured on this page, in the venture. Celebrity Sports Center was the result, and we opened our doors to the public on September 17th, 1960 as a closed corporation.

Walt and Roy Disney were particularly interested in this new venture. They were convinced of the increasing need for family recreation to meet the demands of the people in the rapidly growing Denver area. They also wanted to extend the organization's experience in the areas in which Celebrity would operate. As a result, Celebrity was purchased by Walt Disney Productions in 1962.

The past is prologue to the future. We will still continue to plan to change, add, subtract, and develop Celebrity Sports Center into the kind of family recreation center that Walt Disney envisioned.

1

Photos courtesy of the Celebrity Sports Center Employee Manual

WALT DISNEY   ART LINKLETTER   BURL IVES

CHARLES LAUGHTON   JACK BENNY   JOHN PAYNE

SPIKE JONES   GEORGE BURNS   BING CROSBY

2

Photos courtesy of the Celebrity Sports Center Employee Manual

If all of that wasn't enough to keep visitors busy, a year after the grand opening, the facility opened the largest indoor pool in Colorado, which held 500,000 gallons of heated, filtered water.[14]

Plans were even in place for an on-site hotel in an attempt to make the center a resort destination. If business boomed the way the group anticipated, this concept would pop up in towns across the country.

It sounded like a great time over at the Celebrity Sports Center. Unfortunately, Walt didn't roll a strike with this endeavor.

To celebrate the business's second anniversary, a party was thrown on site. In attendance were Walt, Hayley Mills, Annette Funicello, Pluto, and of course Mickey Mouse. Everyone, including Walt, had on a happy face.

However, behind the scenes, things weren't all fun and joy. The facility was plagued with major management issues. While financially it held its own, it wasn't the cash cow investors had hoped it would be.

Only a year into business, the famous investors were disappointed, restless, and wanted out of the project. Walt started to buy out his celebrity partners, and by late 1962 the business was fully owned by Walt Disney Productions.[15] (This was the name of Walt and Roy's company until the 1980s when it became the Walt Disney Company.)

Not all was lost here for Disney: the business stayed in their portfolio until 1979, when they sold it. Celebrity Sports Center, itself, actually lingered on until June 1994 and, for quite a few years, served as a training ground for Disney's theme park managers.

As Walt's daughter, Diane Disney Miller, said in an interview years later, one of Walt's attorneys, Lloyd Wright, Sr., had approached him with the idea for the project. Walt normally wouldn't go for something like this as he was "wholly concerned with his own projects."[16]

Celebrity Sports Center wasn't the big hit Walt (or his attorney) had hoped it would be. Although, Colorado is closer to the East Coast than Anaheim is, this project wasn't exactly where, or what, Walt had thought his next project should be.

When looking at some of the unrealized yet announced plans from the project—such as hotels and other additions that would make it a destination complex—it's possible to see how this project wasn't merely about bowling, but perhaps something more.

Even down in West Palm Beach with the rejected City of Tomorrow concept, you could see Walt was intrigued by, and mentally flirting with, something on a grander scale than Disneyland.

In late 1961 Walt had Buzz Price conduct another location study centered on the East Coast. This research served to update his three prior studies, one in 1958 and two in 1959.[17]

The studies in 1959 recommended Florida as a prime location for a future Disney project. The study in '61 went a bit further and divided Florida up into five regions.

The regions were compared and contrasted against Walt's needs, which at the time really centered around Walt's one major mandate: "buy a lot of land, something between 5,000 and 10,000 acres."[18] (His Disneyland purchase in 1953 was about 160 acres.)

In addition to his land requirement, Walt didn't want to be too close to the ocean. He didn't want to compete with it for visitors' attention and money. As he once remarked, "We'll make our own lakes and waterways where we want them."[19]

With these two factors, Price's research in '61 determined that central Florida would be the most favorable locale, from around Ocala to areas immediately south of Orlando and anywhere in between, but not near either coast.

Despite Price's encouraging find, Walt still wasn't ready to fully commit to the Sunshine State.

A few more potential projects and proposals trickled into him, all of which were on the East Coast, and some of which he found intriguing.

One project was earmarked for a large parcel of land on the Canadian side of Niagara Falls and involved the Seagram Company.

Guests would be whisked away to several different views and vantage points of the falls. They would board a private railway system along the Niagara River and eventually visit a few Disneyland-like attractions.[20]

The weather would be the biggest obstacle for the project. The cold winters made it easy for Walt to say no to the concept.

A similar weather situation meant the same fate for two other projects, one located at New Jersey's Meadowlands complex just outside of New York City, and the other on a potential site in Washington DC.[21]

This brought things back to Florida, with its year-round warm climate similar to Anaheim's. However, there was still one thing looming in the back of Walt's mind: Could the folks back East really appreciate and enjoy his attractions?

When Disneyland opened, members of the East Coast media didn't exactly "get" what Walt was trying to do.

Jack Lindquist—who was hired in 1955 as the parks advertising and marketing manager—often spoke about his early days on the job at the new concept known as Disneyland. He was quoted about the attitude and resistance he felt from the East Coast:

> *East Coast financiers didn't think Disney's exhibits would appeal to New Yorkers, Lindquist said. "This silly, funny, Mickey Mouse plastic world that works in Anaheim won't ever work in New York" . . . The eastern media just totally pooh-poohed Disneyland. It was the old Lalaland routine: We're too sophisticated. It'll never fly here.*[22]

Walt didn't want another Disneyland concept on his hands where the park only drew regional visitors—or worse, one that would fail all together.

Truth be told, Walt wouldn't even be happy if he drew crowds from the entire state of Florida. He wanted the entire East Coast—and eventually, the entire country—to visit.

Much like the other new projects in his past, there was really only one way to find out how he would fare. He had to jump into the marketplace and see what happened—something he did routinely throughout his life.

A common theme of Walt Disney's career is that he routinely bet big on himself. He didn't care that most people doubted him. History shows he was often short on cash to get his projects going but long on confidence and ingenuity.

He had this experience with the creation of Mickey Mouse; his first full-length animation feature, *Snow White*; and again at Disneyland.

In the early 1960s an opportunity presented itself in which Walt could develop attractions with someone else's money and simultaneously test-market the East Coast with very little risk.

In 1962, WED Enterprises Inc. (WED stood for Walt's initials), which was Disney's research and development arm—today it is known as Walt Disney Imagineering—signed contracts to create, build, and operate exhibits for the 1964–1965 New York World's Fair.

Disney created an exhibit for Pepsi-Cola (in which the company saluted UNICEF), Ford Motor Company, General Electric, and the state of Illinois. To say that the pavilions featuring Disney's exhibits were the most popular is an understatement.

Nearly 47 million people paid to see a Disney production during the twelve-month stint at the fair.[23] Keep in mind the total attendance of the fair was 51.6 million people, so more than 90 percent of fairgoers saw a Disney production—quite impressive.[24]

Each of these exhibits had one thing in common: they featured Walt's new technological marvel—an audio-animatronic.

Whether it was a dinosaur chewing grass, a president sitting down and standing back up, or children singing, these figures started coming to life during Disney's R&D for the world's fair.

This new tech was rooted in government research and development, specifically a segment of magnetic tape technology utilized on the Polaris missile, a two-stage rocket developed during the Cold War. Here's what Walt had to say about it:

It's an offshoot of our work in animation. We started by making the animals move at Disneyland using cams, which can repeat a pattern. Then a whole new area opened up with the release of electronic equipment by the government. Now we can put a whole routine on tape; sound, lip movements, body motions, everything.

The patented process has various degrees of sophistication. They range from one or two simple movements to many complex body actions and facial expressions. "Imagineers" record audible and inaudible sound pulses, music, and dialog on separate magnetic tapes. These are then combined on a single one-inch magnetic tape, which has up to 32 channels or tracks controlling as many as 438 separate actions.

The playback simultaneously relays music and voices to speakers, while sound impulses activate pneumatic and hydraulic valves within the performing figure. Air and fluid tubes and devices expand and contract accordingly to bring about animation. Sound impulses also control stage and theater lighting, permitting an entire show to be controlled from one tape.[25]

At the conclusion of the fair, Walt brought these exhibits back to Disneyland and either featured them as they were in New York or utilized major pieces from them for new in-park experiences.

Any doubts about how the East Coast would receive Walt's attractions were definitively squashed by his success at the fair.

Meanwhile, back at the studio, 1964 was a banner year financially for the company's big screen projects. In August, the film *Mary Poppins* debuted. The movie was a blockbuster and received thirteen Academy Award nominations.

The success of this movie filled the studios coffers with money. Things were shaping up nicely for Walt, Roy, and their next project.

For one of the first times in their storied career, the brothers wouldn't have to scramble for funds, cash in insurance policies, or go into hock to the banks to fund one of Walt's ideas.

And in typical Walt fashion, he let the chips fall where they may and wagered on himself again. He didn't wait to see how his attractions were received at the 1964–1965 New York World's Fair. By late 1963, he had gone full steam ahead on his plans for the state of Florida.

Chapter 3

A LITTLE BIT OF
FLORIDA IN CALIFORNIA

According to Buzz Price's "Preliminary Investigation of Available Acreage for Project Winter," prepared for Walt Disney Productions, ("Project Winter," "Project X," and "Project Future" were just a few of the code names for the Walt's Florida project), "In November of 1961 consensus is that the Ocala area was the optimum geographic location for such a project because of the large number of out-of-state visitors (3.97 million) that passed through or near the city annually."[1]

Walt was no stranger to Ocala—this was Aunt Jessie's territory—and the towns of Paisley, Kismet, and Acron, all in which the Disney family had roots, were in close proximity.

Ocala was the early favorite for the project as land was cheap and plentiful. Probably most crucial to the project, the highways and by-ways were more developed there than other sites in central Florida in 1961.

But a lot had changed in the area since Price's Ocala recommendation, including, most notably, the development of the highways in and around Orlando. Walt was about to see this for himself firsthand.

On November 17, 1963, Walt and his brain trust of executives boarded a borrowed Grumman Gulfstream I private jet—the plane Walt ordered wasn't ready in time, so the Northrop Grumman Corporation lent him one—and set out to comb the East Coast for possible locations for his project.

By the end of the week, the group landed in central Florida to visit Ocala. Walt and crew spent the entire day and night there, hoping the area would check off all the right the boxes, so to speak.

The next morning, Friday, November 22, the group drove to Orlando Executive Airport to fly back home to California.

When Walt entered the plane, he asked the pilot to fly the coasts of the state and circle the center part, keeping the altitude low so he could get a bird's-eye view.

As the plane circled south of Ocala, centering in on Orlando, Walt proclaimed, "That's it!" as he looked down to see major highways coming together.[2]

What he saw was Interstate 4, Interstate 95, and the Sunshine State Parkway. Close proximity to these highways is exactly what his project needed. These roads would allow for unfettered access to his property, not only from the entire state but basically from the entire East Coast.

The search was over, and Walt was feeling good about their trip—they'd pinpointed a location. Before heading back to California, the plane made a stop in New Orleans to refuel.

While on the ground, the group heard horrible news: President John F. Kennedy had been assassinated. The rest of the flight home was spent largely in silence until Walt said to the group before landing, "Well, that's the place—central Florida."[3]

The Disney brothers wasted little time in getting a committee together for land acquisition. Just five days after the trip, Walt and Roy called a top secret meeting, inviting only a handful of their most trusted executives.

Over the next two years, this small group—with the exception of very few additions here and there—were the only people who knew about the Disneys Florida project.

In attendance that day in Conference Room 2E: Card Walker, VP of Marketing; Donn Tatum, also a VP at the time; Jack Sayers, VP for Customer Relations at Disneyland; Larry Tryon, Treasurer; Mel Melton, President of WED Enterprises; Joe Fowler, Disneyland VP of Engineering and Construction; attorney Dick Morrow, VP of Legal; and attorney Robert P. Foster, Assistant Secretary and Legal Counsel for Disneyland.[4]

As Foster recalled in his notes, that first meeting gave a very broad yet defined list of needs for the property:

> It was the consensus of the committee, more accurately it was Walt's wish, with Roy concurring, that the company should undertake a search for a project site in the central Florida region.

> For the purpose of our search the size of the site was arbitrarily set between five and ten thousand acres. I am certain that no one at that first meeting realized what 10,000 acres was in square miles. Nor had any idea how it would be utilized.

> . . . the criteria for the site were that it be of adequate size; the quality of the land, that is it must be useable not swamp land; access to a major highway system with control over the development along the accessway; a local government that would be compatible with the development of the project; attractive indigenous vegetation and a lake were pluses but were not considered essential.[5]

Before the meeting closed, a few final details and precautions were discussed by the group. First, Foster was taking the lead on acquiring the land, which had to be done in absolute secrecy.

If word got out that Disney was poking around Florida looking for thousands of acres, the price would go through the roof, which could derail the project.

Next, in a similar vein, the group had to avoid writing memos about anything relating to the project. Should the event arise that a written memo was in fact needed, copies of the memos would be numbered, returned to, and accounted for by the originator.[6]

Eventually, communication for certain members of the group went even more clandestine. When calling Disney headquarters in California, a relay system was used so their calls went to an office in New York and were then rerouted over to California.[7]

We will see a bit more secrecy moving forward as the story continues, but let's get back to those memos. Obviously, these were the days long before the Internet and email, hence the whole written memo thing for correspondence.

And without Internet, apps like Google Maps did not yet exist, meaning they were unavailable to check out the area of interest in Florida and what, if anything, was surrounding it.

Working from California, over 3,000 miles away from Florida, Foster had his work cut out for him. He came up with three tools to get the lay of the land and rank potential properties without actually being on site.

First, he reached out to the US Geodetic Survey office in Denver, Colorado, so he could obtain the US Geological surveys for the area. These surveys are platted by township, range, and section. They illustrate elevations, waterways and streams, swamps, and tideland areas, along with roads, trails, highways, lakes, existing structures, county and city boundaries, agricultural areas, types of vegetation, military installations, airports, and government owned land.[8]

Second, he utilized the tax assessor's office at the county level to obtain tax assessor maps. In the state of Florida at the time, these maps also contained the name of who owned each parcel of land, along with their address, which eventually proved to be very valuable and time-saving.

Last, to get a feel for the climate of the local real estate market in regard to current prices, recent transactions, and the growth of the community, Foster purchased subscriptions to newspapers in Ocala, Orlando, Lakeland, Tampa, and Kissimmee.

In an effort to keep things secret, neither Foster nor the other members of the committee utilized their own names for these subscriptions. Instead, the names of secretaries, nicknames, initials, and maiden names were used, and the newspapers were sent to post office boxes.[9]

After accumulating and organizing all of this information, Foster started to assemble these data. Most notable were the geodetic maps covering an entire wall—from floor to ceiling—in the secret Disney corporate boardroom in Burbank.

Utilizing the wall of maps, he highlighted the seven-county central Florida area, north to south from Ocala to Kissimmee and east to west from the St. Johns River to the Lakeland area.

At first glance of the map, it looked as though there were about thirty properties that could be of interest to Walt. Further examination brought that number down to about sixteen.

Sites were selected based on Disney's needs and not necessarily whether the property was for sale or not.[10]

Foster accomplished just about all he could from 3,000 miles away. When he first took the lead on the project, he estimated that he could accomplish the land acquisition in about six months.[11]

From his desk in Burbank, he could already see that timeline was too ambitious. While his list of sixteen properties seemed desirable on the surface, many, in fact, could be troublesome.

Some were large, working orange groves that generated a steady income for their owners (at the time, a third of the nation's citrus fruit came from central Florida[12]), so they would likely ask for a premium price, which could mean the properties would be too expensive to purchase.

Other parcels had been poorly subdivided into lots that not only had title problems—most of the owners were scattered throughout the country and difficult to contact—but accessibility problems as well.

Lastly, one of Walt's minor requests was an on-site lake, which many properties had. However, Florida water rights is a complex legal subject, and there was some uncertainty as to whether or not these lakes could be privately owned or if the state had ownership of them, or rights to them.

Foster was very familiar with the real estate laws of California, but laws in Florida were a bit out of his realm. It was time to go on site in hopes of clearing up some of these questions and possibly buying some land.

Foster explained to Walt and Roy that, should he find a parcel that fits their needs, their best course of action was to initially obtain options on the property they wanted rather than outright purchase it.

According to realtor.com:

An option is a contract on a specific piece of real estate that allows the buyer the exclusive right to purchase the property.

Once a buyer has an option to buy a property, the seller cannot sell the property to anyone else. The buyer pays for the option to make this real estate purchase.

The option usually includes a predetermined purchase price and is valid for a specified term such as six months to a year. However, the buyer does not have to buy the property, whereas the seller is obligated to sell to the buyer within the terms of the contract.

Options have to be bought at an agreed-upon price. If the buyer doesn't buy within the time frame, the seller keeps the money used to buy the option.[13]

Going this route gave Foster flexibility in the buying process. Should he have to put several pieces of land together from several different owners to form one large parcel suitable for Disney's needs, the option allowed him the time and exclusivity to do so.

On the other hand, if he couldn't assemble all of the crucial pieces together, Disney could just walk away from the ones Foster had obtained by paying the option price.

This scenario was crucial for the plan, especially from Roy's vantage point. Roy initially stated that they needed to buy the land at a price that could be defended as a sound real estate investment for a public company.

By having the land options, should the project run into trouble, or if plans suddenly changed, Roy wanted to be able to get rid of the acreage without financially hurting the company.[14]

To get the ball rolling and implement these plans, Foster needed to set up a home base in Florida and find a few locals to work with in a real estate and legal capacity.

Naturally, he couldn't reveal too much about the project, or even fully disclose his identity, which could present some challenges. It was time to put the plan into action and head to the South.

Chapter 4

THERE'S A GREAT BIG BEAUTIFUL TOMORROW

On April 20, 1964, Robert Foster attended the New York World's Fair. Still a few days away from opening to the public, he walked the grounds and watched as his boss, Walt Disney, dedicated the State of Illinois exhibit, featuring the audio-animatronic of one of Walt's idols, Abraham Lincoln.

After the dedication Walt, Robert Foster, and a few other Disney employees took in the sights. As the men strolled the grounds, Walt turned to Foster and suggested that he should get a few souvenirs as gifts for his children. Walt said Foster may not have a chance to visit the fair again, then he gave him a sly wink and smile.[1]

Walt was one of the few people at the fair who knew the real reason why Foster was in New York. Roy had arranged for him to meet with Disney's trusted New York legal counsel, Donovan, Leisure, Newton & Irvine.

The law firm's founder, General William J. "Wild Bill" Donovan was great with secrets and strategic planning, as he had been the founding father of the CIA. During the World War II, Donovan helped to create and run the United States Office of Strategic Services (OSS), the precursor to the CIA.

Donovan, however, passed away in 1959, so another partner at the firm, Ralston "Shorty" Irvine, handled the Disney situation.

Irvine vetted an attorney for Foster to meet with in Florida. He also concocted a bit of a backstory for when he encountered new contacts during this whole secret process. He recommended that Foster present himself as being associated with Irvine's firm. (Irvine even went ahead and had business cards made up for Foster.) However, at the last minute, they had to ditch this plan.

Should some curious parties have done a little research into Foster and his firm, they would have seen in *Martindale's Directory of Attorneys* that Disney was one of Donovan, Leisure, Newton & Irvine's clients.[2]

If they dug a little deeper, Robert Foster would show up in the Disney annual report to shareholders. It was a long shot, but they couldn't take the chance of someone making this connection. [3]

Another law practice, Burke & Burke, not too far from Irvine's firm, would be used as Foster's cover. The firm agreed to let him use their name and address, along with receiving his telephone messages, as long as "it was nothing that would embarrass them."[3]

Foster's backstory was set, and an arrangement had been made for him to meet with the Irvine-vetted attorney in Florida. Foster left New York City the next morning and landed in Miami on April 21, 1964. His meeting with Attorney Paul L. E. Helliwell took place that afternoon.

It had been quite easy for Irvine to recommend Helliwell. He was a native Floridian and had a very impressive background.

Helliwell had been a member of Wild Bill Donovan's OSS team and had controlled intelligence operations in regions of Japan, China, and what was once known as Burma and Indochina.[4]

Here's a description of Helliwell from a sanitized CIA document released via the Freedom of Information Act:

The gruff Mr. Helliwell, 62 when he died on Christmas Eve, 1976, from emphysema complications, was no stranger to the murky world of spying. During World War II, he was chief of special intelligence in China for the Office of Strategic Services, or OSS, the forerunner of the CIA.

Colleagues from those days recall that Mr. Helliwell, then a colonel, regularly used to buy information with five-pound shipments of opium. ("three sticky brown bars," according to one man). They also say he ran an operation code named "Deer

Mission" in which OSS personnel secretly parachuted into Indochina to treat Ho Chi Minh for malaria.

In 1951, Mr. Helliwell helped set up and run Sea Supply Corp, a concern controlled by the CIA as front. For almost 10 years, Sea Supply was used to supply huge amounts of weapons and equipment to 10,000 Nationalist Chinese troops in Burma as well as Thailand's police.

One former federal official who helped scrutinize Sea Supply says, "it was one of the CIA's finance channels for operations against Cuba." Mr. Helliwell reputedly was one of the paymasters for the ill-fated Bay of Pigs invasion in 1961, as well as other "extensive" CIA operations throughout Latin America.

In particular, the former federal official says Mr. Helliwell was "deeply involved" in financing a series of covert forays between 1964 and 1975 against Cuba by CIA operatives working from Andros Island, the largest of the Bahamian Islands.[5]

Sheesh, I feel like I should be writing a book about Paul Helliwell and not about Disney! Welp, it looks like in the midst of trying to topple Cuba, Helliwell helped Disney buy some land and set up its own regime in Florida. It was pretty obvious that Disney's secret would be safe with Helliwell.

Back in Miami, Helliwell the civilian was a sharp attorney and owner of the Mercantile Bank and Trust Company, Castle Bank & Trust, and American Bankers Insurance—it was eventually revealed that Castle Bank & Trust also led back to the CIA.

It appeared as though for Walt and Roy, the adage "it's not what you know, it's who you know," rang true for them on this project. Helliwell was an excellent "fixer" and left an indelible mark on their project. As you'll read, one could even argue that Walt Disney World wouldn't have happened on the land it currently resides on without Paul L. E. Helliwell.

(S)   SECRET CONFIDENTIAL

CENTRAL INTELLIGENCE AGENCY
WASHINGTON 25, D. C.

OCT 26 1949

(b)(3)

APPROVED FOR
RELEASE☐DATE:
23-Apr-2008

The Director
Federal Bureau of Investigation
Tenth & Pennsylvania Ave., N. W.
Washington 25, D. C.

Attention: Mr. Christopher Callan

Re: Request for Investigation

Dear Sir:

It is requested that an investigation of the following named person be
conducted in order to determine loyalty, character, discretion, trustworthiness,
financial habits, foreign connections, and general suitability for Government
employment:

Name	Reference
HELLIWELL, Paul Lionel Edward	21663

The above-named person:
(X) Has been employed as an intermittent consultant by this Agency since 6/27/49.
( ) Is an applicant for employment.
( ) Was employed _____ and has no access to classified information.
( ) Was employed _____ on unclassified duties in cover status.
( ) Has been a full employee of this Agency since _____.
( ) Will be (Was) employed under cover designation (on _____).
No CIA interest should be indicated during the investigation.
Such portion of the completed investigation report as may
indicate CIA connection should, under no circumstances, be
disclosed to a third party without the prior approval of this
Agency. Likewise, administrative detail, in connection with
this investigation, should be so handled as to afford main-
tenance of the necessary cover.

Remarks: Limited investigation by Hooper-Holmes in 1944 disclosed no derogatory
information.

It is requested that the attached PHS be returned with your report.

SE 2

RECORDED

50 OCT 27 1949

b2

FOR THE CHIEF OF INSPECTION AND SECURITY STAFF:

ERNAL F. GEISS
Chief, Personnel Security Division
Branch

Enc. - 1 PHS

Form No. 38-103
Feb 1949

SECRET   CONFIDENTIAL

1072252

Courtesy of the Central Intelligence Agency

But back to Foster's first meeting with Helliwell. At 1:00 p.m. on April 21, 1964, the two men met at the law office of Helliwell, Melrose & DeWolf. Let's read about it from Foster in his own words:

> I explained that I represented a large corporate client, public, on the New York Stock Exchange, who was interested in acquiring a large parcel of land, as much as 10,000 acres in the central part of the state, for use as the site for a development that did not exist now in Florida, that the project would have an economic impact on the area establish new businesses and create substantial employment. Probably it would create a wave of speculation in real estate in the area selected.
>
> We had decided, for reasons that I would explain later, that confidentiality was essential and that was one of the reasons for selecting an attorney away from the immediate area of the prospective site.
>
> Time would be of the essence once a site or sites were selected. Indications were that numerous parcels would be involved in the acquiring of the site. I explained that we had conducted a preliminary investigation and had developed a plan for proceeding that contemplated engaging both an attorney and a real estate consultant.
>
> We would expect that the attorney would make recommendations and assist us in the selection of the consultant. Probably until such time as a sound relationship was established, we should remain as an undisclosed principal to the consultant.[6]

After hearing all of that, Helliwell stepped out for an hour to attend a previously scheduled meeting. When their meeting resumed, Foster asked if Helliwell would be interested in taking on the project.

Despite Helliwell's knowledge that Foster came to him as a referral from the highly regarded Donovan firm, Foster immediately sensed reluctance and resistance from him. As a fellow skeptic and attorney, Foster could appreciate that.

Apparently, Helliwell couldn't put his suspiciousness, or at least his curiousness, aside. Foster sensed that he wouldn't agree to come aboard without knowing more, or at least knowing who the client was.

Quickly, Foster reflected and put himself into Helliwell's shoes. He ruminated that, as an attorney himself, he would have the same doubts and reluctance to blindly move forward.

In fact, if Helliwell did take on this project without more information, Foster would have been very suspicious of *his* judgement.[7]

Foster then proceeded to do exactly what he said he wouldn't during the project's initial meeting—he divulged the truth to Helliwell. He explained that he represented Walt Disney Productions. They weren't looking to put a studio in central Florida but rather something along the lines of Disneyland, perhaps.

He went further, saying they were only in the concept stages at that point and the project wasn't fully defined. Helliwell promptly accepted Disney as a client.

Looking back decades later, here's what Foster had to say about his decision to disclose who he was, and who he was representing, during his first meeting with Helliwell:

I had no doubts or regrets over the decision to disclose our identity to Paul Helliwell when I did, it was the correct and proper thing to do. There was an obvious release of apprehension when the mystery of our identity was eliminated from the discussion.

Not only were Paul Helliwell and his partners, Mary Jane Melrose and Tom DeWolf eminently qualified as attorneys, they were a limitless source of sound council and advice. Strong friendships had their founding on that occasion.

Paul Helliwell was one of the few who overcame the stigma of being an attorney, and was accepted into the inner circle of admiration, respect and friendship with Walt Disney. To

Roy Disney, he became a very special confidant, counselor and friend.[8]

The week following their initial meeting, Helliwell arranged for a confab between Foster and his real estate consultant, Roy Hawkins.

Hawkins was another well-connected businessman who had worked in the Florida real estate scene for over forty years, primarily in property management and development.

At the time of his meeting with Foster, Hawkins was a vice president with Beesemer Properties, which was a real estate holding company under the trust of the Henry Phipps Jr. estate.

Phipps Jr. was a co-founder of Carnegie Steel with Andrew Carnegie. In 1901 the two men sold their steel company to United States Steel for $400 million.

Phipps Jr. took his cut—roughly $48 million—and started buying up miles and miles of land heading from Palm Beach, Florida, down to Miami. Hawkins helped to manage this portfolio, and he also had a hand in developing Miami's Biscayne Boulevard.[9]

When Helliwell approached Hawkins with the project, he too was skeptical of coming aboard. He noted that Florida's real estate history was littered with scams and shady land deals of people selling swampland out of the back of magazines (we will see more of this soon, as there is a Disney tie-in).

Without more information, Hawkins didn't want to join the project. But Helliwell wouldn't relent; he promised Foster he wouldn't disclose Disney's identity, and in turn, Helliwell assured Hawkins that he wouldn't get him into something that he would regret. Hawkins took Helliwell at his word.

With Hawkins in the fold, the introductions were made. Helliwell, Hawkins, and Bob Price sat down for their first meeting—yes, that isn't a typo, Bob Price (not to be confused with Buzz Price either).

From this meeting on—and with all new contacts made in Florida going forward—Robert Foster dropped his last name to protect his true identity and utilized his middle name, Price, as his last name instead (he is still referred to by his actual last name throughout the rest of the book).

Foster gave Hawkins his list of wants and needs for the central Florida area and let him get to work. The men would meet again in Miami—now the home base for the project—when Foster returned from his first scouting trip in central Florida.

While in the Orlando area, Foster drove the roads of sleepy central Florida, surveying locations. He saw lots of cattle, swamps, and more orchards and cypress trees than he had ever seen before. What he didn't see was a lot of possibilities for the land he encountered.

He did bump into a familiar face, a fellow employee, if you will.

When he approached Haines City, he passed a processing plant owned by the Florida Citrus Cooperative. Donald Duck's face was painted on the wall—the cooperative was an orange juice licensee of Walt Disney Productions.[10]

If Donald's face was a welcome sight, there were a few other faces that weren't. As Foster recalled, he didn't want to stand out or draw any more attention to himself than necessary. He worked on his phonetics for when it was time to speak to the locals:

> *"I could pronounce 'Toe-hope-a-ka-loga' as in the Florida lake. But my fragile façade was broken when a service station attendant volunteered, 'You ain't a native. Where you from?'"*
> *He had goofed. He asked how far it was to "Kiss-a-me" (Kissimmee), as opposed to "Ka-sim-ee." "My first lesson on the rules of behavior: Listen, don't talk."*[11]

As Foster continued to canvas the area, he worked down his list of sixteen possible sites. Most sites were coming off the list, and very few were staying on. He noticed one thing the area had in common with Disneyland: oranges.

But while that park is built on what was once an orange grove, he didn't think the same thing would happen in Florida—unless there was a drastic freeze in the near future.

His research told him that the price of a commercial citrus grove was not based on the price of the land but rather the production of each tree as a production unit; the groves he came across were thriving.[12]

After two full days in the area south of Orlando, he felt as though nearly all of the sites he saw were undesirable. He had one more spot to look over, and then he would head up to north of Orlando and the area around Lake Monroe.

Foster finally liked what he saw at the last site south of Orlando. The property was owned by two members of the Demetree family, along with a partner.

It was 12,400 acres and could be purchased as one complete and continuous tract of land. He wouldn't have to deal with trying to piece together multiple properties to achieve the 10,000 acres Walt and Roy were seeking.

The location was prime as well, as it was close to Interstate 4 and Florida's Turnpike. Initially, it seemed as though there was one problem, not necessarily a major problem, but more of a nuisance.

Foster's preliminary research revealed a number of small parcels within and along the tract that had an assortment of owners.

From 1911 to 1913, much of this land had been subdivided into five-acre parcels and sold through mail order via advertisements in the back of magazines and newspapers across the country. A five-dollar down payment and five dollars per month bought a five-acre farm. The parcels were sold under the name Munger Farms.

According to Foster, the draftsman who created this Munger subdivision on paper probably never saw the property—and neither did most of the buyers. The lots were in odd shapes and often within lakes or swamps, making them inaccessible.

Reaching out to these property owners, wherever they were (and assuming they were still alive), and persuading all of them to sell could be a nightmare.

The Price and Location of

THE MUNGER FARMS

Make them Ideal Homes or Investments.

Have you selected yours? If not use the following Application:

MONTHLY PAYMENT APPLICATION.

WILLIS R. MUNGER, 517 Francis St., St. Joseph, Mo.

Dear Sir:Find enclosed $.........as first payment by me on a.........
acre Munger Farm in Orange County, Florida. I agree to make further
monthly payments, as per your schedule, until my farm has been paid for.
The price is to be $20 per acre, without interest or extra charges of any
kind, and you will guarantee title and pay all taxes until I have completed
my payments.

In making remittances, please follow the schedule given here:

$ 5.00 cash and $ 5.00 per month buys a five-acre farm.
10.00 cash and 7.00 per month buys a ten-acre farm.
20.00 cash and 10.00 per month buys a twenty-acre farm.
40.00 cash and 20.00 per month buys a forty-acre farm.

You are given immediate possession without signing further agreements
as soon as you have made a single payment on your farm.

Name... ... ...

Address... ... ...
Or call on LEN J. MUNGER, the Orlando Representative,

Office With C. S. McEwen, 3 Doors South of Postoffice.

Courtesy of the *Orlando Evening Star*, January 6, 1911

Foster gave the property high marks for just about everything, but he really wanted to steer clear of buying it. Getting ownership and clear titles to these Munger Farms lots could be an exercise in futility.[13]

It appeared as though this part of central Florida wouldn't work for the project. Perhaps Hawkins was successful in putting together a list of properties which better fit their needs.

It was well into May when Foster went back to Miami to meet with Hawkins and Helliwell. Hawkins confirmed that he had a list of properties to check out.

Helliwell wasn't able to make the site visit so his partner Tom DeWolf took his place.

Roy Hawkins, Tom DeWolf, and Robert Foster (AKA Bob Price) took a trip to Orlando. It must have been an interesting car ride up: DeWolf knew Foster by his given name, while Hawkins knew him as Bob Price.[14]

The first stop the group made was in Daytona, where they paid a visit to two sites. The first was the 10,000-acre Oak Hill Ranch. The second was the 75,000-acre Tomoka Ranch.

Oak Hill had possibilities, but Foster really liked the Tomoka property. The land only had one owner, so the negotiations would be direct and straightforward.

Either the entire parcel or any part of it could be purchased. Walt was looking for a lot of natural vegetation and a lake or two. This property had both, along with the Tomoka River running through it.

The location was in proximity to Interstate 95, which fulfilled the access point the project needed. Foster thought this could be the one.

Another property Hawkins found was just south of Orlando. As it turned out, it was the previously visited Demetree tract. Foster told Hawkins he liked it but cringed thinking about having to clear up all the issues with the old Munger lots.

The three men took a tour of the property anyway, this time with the Demetrees. The men covered the entire tract, from Bay Lake to Reedy Creek.

Hawkins, DeWolf, and Foster liked everything they saw, but as Foster commented at the time, "It was the intangibles that caused the misgivings."[15]

They thanked the Demetrees for their time, and both parties went their own way. Hawkins was interested in looking around the vicinity of the Demetree tract. He nudged Foster and DeWolf to drive down a few backroads.

As they drove along, in the middle of nowhere, they came upon a large, well-maintained, two-story white house facing a lake and surrounded by orange groves.

They thought the house was probably built in the late 1910s or early 1920s. Hawkins wanted to get out of the car and check out the house—Foster and DeWolf, not so much.

Hawkins persisted and decided to go knock on the door. An older woman answered. She and Hawkins chatted for about five or ten minutes. Then all of a sudden Hawkins started to run off of the porch. The older woman chased behind as she repeatedly hit him with a broom.

Hawkins had just met Mrs. Higley, who followed him to the car and rambled on that "the last no good man she had on the place ran away, and she wouldn't have another man on the place if he had diamonds on his back."[16]

As the three men pulled away, Hawkins said that he complimented Mrs. Higley on how great her place looked. They engaged in some small talk about her citrus orchard, and everything seemed fine until she inquired about who he was.

He told her he was a real estate man from Miami, and then *poof*, she exploded on him. He said he should have known better. He probably should have said he was a brush salesman from Valdosta, Georgia and then the men probably would have been invited in for dinner![17]

With Mrs. Higley in their rearview, Foster felt good about the progress they had made. He thought the Tomoka location in Daytona could be perfect and an easy acquisition. It was time to go back to California and share his findings with Walt and Roy.

In late May 1964, Foster was back in the boardroom in Burbank to give a presentation to Walt, Roy, and a small group of executives. As a result of the trip, he had accordingly updated the big map on the wall.

Foster went over the properties, giving the pros and cons of each. He thought it all came down to three properties out of the original sixteen: the Demetree tract, the Bronson tract (which was near the

Demetree tract—he had seen the land but wasn't able to get a meeting with the owners), and the Tomoka Ranch property in Daytona.

Foster's favorite was the Tomoka property. As he made eye contact with Walt and Roy, he pitched hard for it. Then he started to get a bad feeling. Let's hear it directly from Robert Foster:

> *I sensed a certain uneasiness. Then came the unequivocal signal of Walt's disapproval. Walt always telegraphed his punches of disapproval, no words, no gestures, just an arched left eyebrow. If you were speaking, had the floor, or otherwise were engaged in something that got his attention and that left eyebrow went up, you were in trouble. I was in trouble.*
>
> *Walt commented "Bob, what the hell are you doing way up there?" He approached the map and pointed to a tract of land near the I-4 and 535 interchange, right in the heart of the dreaded Munger subdivision area, an area that I by no means intended to recommend. Walt said, "This is where we can do some development of a conventional nature."*[18]

And with that, the meeting was over. The property of his nightmares was the property of Walt's dreams.

The area Walt pointed to was in the vicinity of the Demetree property and the Bronson property—neither Hawkins nor Foster were even sure if it was for sale—and a few other smaller tracts.

It was going to be a big task to gather all of those properties and then sort out the title issues on the smaller Munger parcels.

No sense in complaining; it was time to get to work. Walt and Roy wanted those properties, so back to Florida Foster went to make his first land purchase.

Chapter 5

THE BLESSING OF SIZE

By June of 1964, Foster was back in Miami to negotiate for the Demetree tract. He never flew directly into or out of Miami, or directly into or out of Southern California. To conceal his plans, he often made stops in the Midwest, sometimes in Kansas to see his mother.[1]

Joining him in Miami were Donn Tatum and Roy Disney. They were staying at the Dupont Plaza Hotel. When they arrived, Roy assumed the name Roy Davis, as it matched the initials on his luggage.

Just as "Mr. Davis" turned away from the registration desk in the lobby, someone began repeatedly shouting his name, Roy Disney.

Roy moved as fast as he could across the lobby to stifle the voice. He gave the man a big embrace and whispered to him, "Don't say my full name, I just registered under an alias."

The man shouting was Elliott Levitas, an attorney who had done work for the Disneys from time to time. More recently, he had become a United States Congressman for the state of Georgia.

Since Roy already knew Helliwell, there was no need to use the Roy Davis moniker with him. However, he did utilize it briefly with Hawkins, until the two started chatting.

Both Roy and Hawkins had been in the military during World War I. As they kibitzed about their past, they realized they had a shared connection. As it turned out, Roy had worked for Hawkins's Uncle in Kansas City when he was employed as a bank teller.[2] It really was a small world after all.

Roy was in town to give the green light for the Demetree tract. The property was roughly five-and-one-half miles from north to south and about three miles wide from west to east.[3]

Hawkins got the ball rolling with the Demetrees—Bill and Jack—and their partner, Bill Jenkins. He informed them of his interested party. Hawkins also planted the seed that the property had a slew of problems, which made it somewhat undesirable.

If a deal were to happen, it would only take place once all of the issues from the Munger subdivision were resolved.

The following week, all parties met in Jacksonville at the Demetrees' attorney's office. Before negotiations started, it was disclosed that, should they come to an agreement, Helliwell was putting the contract into his name as the trustee for an undisclosed principle.

When pressed on the issue, Helliwell assured them that the principle was of the highest level and a public company. Nothing more could be said, as it could jeopardize the entire project if word leaked out to the press.[4]

Negotiations commenced, and they did not go smoothly. They started at 8:00 a.m., and by 7:00 p.m., there was still no agreement in place.

Helliwell took the negotiating position that, on paper, the land was a mess. It appeared as though in addition to the Munger troubles, there was a bigger problem.

The Demetrees didn't own the mineral rights to the land and without them, the property was useless.[5]

Helliwell figured it could take up to a year to untangle the Munger lots, and in regard to this new, even larger problem, they might never be able to secure the property's mineral rights.

The Demetrees countered and said the property was sold "as is," and that's why it was reasonably priced. They offered to help acquire the rights—though they had tried before and had been unsuccessful—but ultimately the effort and cost would be on the buyer.

By the twelfth hour of negotiations, an agreement was reached to option the property. The terms were a six-month option at a cost of $25,000. Should Helliwell eventually purchase the property, the price would be at $145 an acre (the Demetrees and Jenkins had originally asked for $165).[6]

As explained previously, this option took the property off the market and gave exclusive buying rights to Disney. During the option period, the company would try to obtain the mineral rights and attempt to purchase any adjacent property Walt and his team felt was needed, along with sorting through the Munger issues.

If they were unable to get the other properties, or fail in acquiring the mineral rights, they would pay the $25,000 and move on from the deal.

With their first parcel in the fold, it was time to obtain the mineral rights, also known as the underground rights.

The Demetrees and Jenkins were builders and land speculators. In 1960 they purchased this tract for less than $100 an acre from cattleman and state senator Irlo Bronson Sr.[7] So why would they be in such a hurry to sell it just four years later?

Well, it's probably not a great idea to build on a parcel of land whose surface could be destroyed by another party—this was the case with the Demetree property.

Back in the day, Florida separated mineral rights from land ownership. Basically, this meant that land ownership could be divided horizontally and vertically.[8]

In the central part of the state, this division was primarily done to mine for phosphorous—today, roughly 80 percent of the phosphorous used in the United States still comes from this area.[9]

This was the situation the Demetrees and Jenkins, and now the Disney brothers, faced. In the early 1900s, Tufts University, in Massachusetts, owned roughly 25,000 acres in the area of what would become the Demetree property. During the 1940s, Tufts started to sell the surface rights and retain ownership of the mineral rights.

The owner of the mineral rights could enter the property, explore it, and then start to mine it. They could build roads, knock down any structures, or just blow everything up on the surface, despite not having ownership of the surface rights.[10]

As Jack Demetree commented years later when asked about his property, he said, "Nobody wanted to buy the land when [Tufts] could come in and tear down houses to get to the minerals."[11]

Helliwell, Foster, and Hawkins hoped to pry these rights away from the University, but it wasn't going to be easy.

Tufts's contract seemed rock solid; it stated they owned the rights forever. While trying to untangle the Tufts mess, though, Foster discovered that additional rights to the property had been sold.

At some point in the past, Wilson Cypress Incorporated bought a ninety-nine-year lease to the rights for the cypress trees.

There was also a third rights owner in the mix: the Hercules Powder Company had the rights to harvest the timber and stumps. They were allowed to come onto the property, remove the timber and stumps, and grind them down to dust, which they then used to manufacture explosive powder.[12]

Clearly, these ownership rights were crucial for Disney to move forward. But truth be told, the Demetrees probably wanted Disney to buy the rights even more so than the Disneys themselves, as this could be the best chance for the Demetrees and Jenkins to unload the property.

If the Disneys didn't get the rights or the land, they would move on. As for the Demetrees, they had a $90,000 payment due in the near future—and still no mineral rights.[13]

Foster went headfirst into research to see what, if anything, was actually underground. This would give Disney an idea about how to plan negotiations with Tufts University.

Foster contacted Florida's Geological Office, as state law mandated that permits must be acquired to explore for minerals in the state. As it turned out, the property had already been explored for phosphorous. Some had been found, but the quantity wasn't enough to mine. Sun Oil Company (known as Sunoco today) had also explored the site for oil. The company's results were negative as well.

Foster took copies of these reports and went to work. If there were no minerals or oil underground, why would the rights holders continue to hold onto the rights? This simplistic, common sense question was the plan of attack for Tufts University.

But first, Foster had to deal with Hercules Powder's timber and stumps rights. The company was still actively removing stumps from the property, but they agreed to a buyout and asked for some time to remove their equipment.[14]

Next up was Wilson Cypress. It appeared as though, at that point, the company was more interested in making money selling the rights they owned than harvesting the cypress trees. There was no negotiation needed, as the company had a fee schedule—pay the fee and obtain the release, done and done.[15]

It was now time to deal with Tufts. While there was nothing of value underground, the university really didn't have much incentive to sell the rights, let alone listen to a pitch from someone seeking to pry them away.

Foster and Helliwell researched the Tufts Board of Trustees and Finance Committee. None of the names looked familiar to them, but one of the members of the committee was a vice president at the First National Bank of Boston.

As luck would have it, Helliwell had a friend who had been a fellow colonel and officer in the OSS and was now the president of the First National Bank of Boston.[16]

A quick phone call to his old buddy confirmed that a gentleman with the last name of Keesler was a VP at the bank and was on Tufts's board. The connection was made, and an introduction was in the works.

The door had been opened for Helliwell and Foster, but they still had to walk through it and close the deal. A strategy was developed, and here's what it distilled down to.

Private colleges and universities need money; they are always looking for ways to make it. This could be a great monetary opportunity for Tufts if they recognized the scenario being presented to them and seized it.

Helliwell and Foster framed Tufts's mineral rights' ownership as such: the university was holding a commodity of questionable value that may or may not—most likely not—yield a return on investment.

Judging by the survey from Florida's Geological Office, there were no significant minerals or deposits which would make them money. It would therefore be a poor business decision for the university to hold on to the rights. Rather they should sell them immediately for cash.[17]

Here was the package presented to the board: Helliwell would buy 50 percent of Tufts's mineral rights, along with a complete release of rights to enter the property and explore it.

Tufts could retain the other 50 percent interest as a hedge against minerals ever being extracted.[18]

Since the mineral rights Tufts owned were spread over some 20,000 acres, there was a good chance the university owned the rights to the property adjacent to the Demetree tract, and Disney may want to purchase some of those parcels as well.[19]

This scenario was arranged as a two-fold measure. First, Disney certainly may buy more land and encounter Tufts again. Second, this assured Tufts additional money. If Disney bought more land, the company would exercise an option on the second 50 percent of the rights; if not, Tufts would get paid on the option not exercised.[20]

Helliwell and Foster thought this was a great offer, one that Tufts couldn't walk away from.

There was also one more calculated twist from Helliwell and Foster. As the Demetrees stated, it was up to the buyers to spend their time and money to obtain the mineral rights.

As Disney's attorneys saw it, the mineral rights could be really valuable regardless of what happened in the purchase from the Demetrees. I'll let Foster explain it:

From our point, if we didn't exercise the Demetree option, the Demetrees were obliged to acquire the mineral rights from us.

They would be anxious to do so, since they had been trying to acquire the mineral rights since purchasing the property.

If we acquired the mineral rights on property we did not own, we would sell them to recover our costs.[21]

The meeting with Tufts took place at the First National Bank of Boston. Helliwell had the Demetrees go in first and make a personal and passionate plea.

They stated their case and explained that they had an agreement to sell the property. If they didn't get the release, their deal would fall through, and that could be financially devastating to them.

The board of trustees heard their plea and immediately replied with a big fat *no*. Tufts wasn't budging on their ownership of the rights.

Since that route didn't work, Helliwell decided to join the meeting. He hit Tufts with what he called the "ultimate paradox presentation." Here's how he framed it:

That which appears to be of value is actually pernicious, if of value only by reason of its elimination. Based on evidence, the letters of exploration reports there are no minerals to give royalty value to the mineral rights reservations.

If there are no minerals the remaining feature of the reservation is the right to enter upon the land but then only to explore for non-existent minerals.

The right of entry then is a right without purpose, but if that feature of the reservation has any value it is the value the landowner will pay for its release, to eliminate the right of entry from reservation.

The amount that will be paid to the release and eliminate them depends on the value of the land they encumber.

The value of the land depends on its present and prospective use. The reservation of rights of entry onto the property and exploration are so onerous and restrictive that so long as they remain in effect, the land use will be so limited that it will always be of low value.

The opportunity now being offered to the trustees is to end this perpetual condition by releasing the reservations on the land we want to purchase. By doing so the value of land in the area, on which they have reservations of mineral rights will have a good prospect of increasing in value, and with it an increase in what a landowner will pay for their release.

Their continuing to hold the mineral rights as a commodity in their present form would defeat their objective of enhancing the college's endowment.[22]

Dang, that was a mouthful, but also a very pointed and succinct argument for selling—which is what Tufts did. The next morning the paperwork was signed. Tufts gave up their mineral rights for $15,000.[23]

As predicted, eventually the surrounding land went up in price, and Tufts was able to increase their asking price for mineral rights on the other parcels they owned.

Tufts even hit up the Demetrees for a generous contribution to the university's endowment as part of the agreement.[24]

The Demetree tract in place, there were two other significant parcels that Foster and Helliwell felt they must get under contract.

Merely owning the Demetree tract could leave Walt with the potential for another Disneyland situation—encroachment on his land by others. The adjacent Bay Lake property and the Hamrick tract both touched the Demetree Property and needed to be purchased, if for nothing else, as a buffer.

The Bay Lake property was owned by a social–sporting group of approximately thirteen married couples. This meant Foster and

Helliwell had to get a lot of people to agree to the same thing, which is often a challenge. Potentially adding to the challenge was the fact that this group used their land often and enjoyed it.[25]

The Bay Lake tract was about 1,250 acres and included most of the lake and much of the lake frontage. As mentioned earlier, Walt really wanted a lake, but a quick survey of Florida laws made him a bit nervous to dip in his toe.[26]

Foster's initial research back in California revealed that lakes the size of Bay Lake could be considered "meander lakes," which meant the lake was usually owned by the state.

If the state owned it, they also controlled who had access to it and what could be done there (i.e., open it up to the public for boating, fishing, swimming, etc.).

In the case of Bay Lake, this would be right next to Disney's property. If the state opened it up to recreation for the public, Walt would not be happy.[27]

Foster's research while in Florida revealed the lake wasn't on the state's official list of meandered lakes. However, he wouldn't know that with absolute certainty until he could connect with the ownership group.

Contact was made with the owners, and the lake was, in fact, privately owned. Although it wasn't officially listed for sale, Foster made an offer to purchase it.

After several weeks of sitting on the offer, the couples came to a decision: they would sell. The Bay Lake property sold for $250,000.

The next "must-have" property was the Hamrick tract. This tract was specifically the land Walt touched on the map when he had become aggravated with Foster for pushing the property up in Daytona.[28]

These 2,700 acres owned by the Hamrick family were primarily used to grow citrus. In July 1964, the family put the property up for sale. By September of 1964 the Disney brothers were the new owners, having paid $623,523 for it.[29]

Things were moving along nicely by the fall of 1964. But for Disney to have one large cohesive tract, there was still a slew of smaller properties to purchase.

As mentioned previously, some of this land was located inside the Demetree tract, while other portions ran adjacent to it. These were the small, often five-acre, parcels that had originally been purchased from Munger Farms out of the back of magazines and newspapers.

The entire Munger Farms subdivision was a disaster, both on paper and in person. Subdividing land today requires engineers, surveyors, planners, and attorneys, but back when Mr. Munger owned the land, it appeared as though he—or someone he hired—took the map of his land and drew rectangles across the entire property. Each rectangle was a parcel for sale.[30]

No actual survey was done, so in reality, on the ground, each piece of land was not really a rectangle but a trapezoid, due to the earth's physical features.

Technically, the Orange County government recognized these parcels as the Munger subdivision. Disney not only wanted to own all of these parcels, but he wanted the legality of the subdivision dissolved.

One way to achieve this was to buy all of the land in the subdivision and petition the county government to have it dissolved, which is what Foster set out to do.

The folks who owned these parcels were living all over the country. Often, they were the original owners dating back to the early 1900s.

There were too many owners for Foster to deal with himself, so Hawkins outsourced the task of acquisition to a company named Florida Ranch Lands.

Florida Ranch Lands tracked down as many owners as they could. Once located, the owners were asked if they wanted to sell their little pieces of Florida—this was done primarily by phone.

R E S O L U T I O N

VACATING A PORTION OF THE MUNGER LAND COMPANY SUB-

DIVISION PLAT IN SECTION 31, TOWNSHIP 24 SOUTH, RANGE

28 EAST.

Upon motion by Commissioner Cooper, seconded by Commissioner Evans,

and unanimously carried, the following Resolution was adopted by the Board

of County Commissioners of Orange County, Florida, on the 1st day of

August, A. D., 1966, to-wit:

WHEREAS, pursuant to the provisions of Sections 192.29 and 192.30,

Florida Statutes, a petition was filed with the Board of County Commissioners

of Orange County, Florida, to vacate a portion of the plat of the Munger Land

Company Subdivision on file in Plat Book E, pages 3, 7, 22 and 23, Public Re-

cords of Orange County, Florida, as follows:

> Lots 8 through 12, 17 through 27, 38 through 57, 62, 65, 68
> through 88, 90, 91, 93, 103 through 120 and 125 through 128
> of Munger Land Company Subdivision of Section 31, Township
> 24 South, Range 28 East, according to the plat thereof on file
> in Plat Book "E", page 22, Public Records of Orange County,
> Florida,

by Reedy Creek Ranch, Inc., a Florida Corporation, Tomahawk Properties,

Inc., a Florida corporation, William E. Potter, Julia G. Switlick and Philip

N. Smith, and

WHEREAS, the said Reedy Creek Ranch, Inc. is the fee simple owner

of Lots 8 through 12, 19 through 27, 38 through 57, 65, 70 through 88, 90, 91,

103 through 120 and 125 through 128, all in Section 31, and

WHEREAS, the said Tomahawk Properties, Inc. is the fee simple

owner of Lots 17, 18 and 62 of said Section 31, covered by the plat of the Munger

Land Company Subdivision sought to be vacated, and

WHEREAS, the said William E. Potter is the fee simple owner of

Lot 68 of said Section 31, of said plat sought to be vacated, and

WHEREAS, the said Julia G. Switlick is the fee simple owner of Lot

69 of said Section 19, of said plat sought to be vacated, and

WHEREAS, the said Philip N. Smith is the fee simple owner of

Lot 93 of said Section 31 of said plat sought to be vacated, and

WHEREAS, the above described property does not lie within the muni-

cipal limits of any city in Orange County, Florida, and

WHEREAS, none of the streets or alleys in the plat of the Munger

Land Company Subdivision sought to be vacated have been taken over by the

County for maintenance and are not part of the county road system and they

serve no useful purpose to any of the public except the Petitioners, and

If there was no response over the phone, a letter was mailed. If the letter didn't get a response, Foster usually made an in-person sales call to the last known address of the person who owned the property in question.

His sales calls took him to California, Montana, Iowa, Texas, Tennessee, Ohio, Colorado, Rhode Island, Illinois, Kansas, Indiana, Pennsylvania, and New York.

Munger had sold a good deal of land to folks who never saw their parcel, let alone visited the state of Florida.[31] The stories of how some people obtained their lots was often pretty interesting.

In Iowa, Foster encountered two middle-aged sisters who weren't very forthright or comfortable speaking about how their family obtained their parcel. However, they were willing to sell their twenty acres, which is now part of Walt Disney World's Fort Wilderness Resort.[32]

As the sale was completed, Foster started to leave the house when he was approached by a third sibling, a brother. He said their father had won the land in a high-stakes poker game in Texas. The sisters were hesitant to talk about this as they didn't want to admit that they might be sharing in an ill-gotten gain.[33]

While in Iowa, Foster also met a sweet widower in her eighties, Mrs. Rose. Her husband had been a mining engineer who hadn't been very good with money. He repeatedly blew through any savings he could accumulate. This drove Mrs. Rose crazy and made her nervous about her future.

She decided to scrimp on the family groceries and cut a few corners financially wherever she could. Once she accumulated a bit of savings, she decided to invest in real estate. She purchased a Munger lot in her own name without her husband knowing.

She too agreed to sell her lot but with one stipulation: Foster had to escort her to a day at Disneyland—an obligation he fulfilled.[34]

Not everyone was eager to sell their land. One such owner was Mrs. Eassey, from Fort Lauderdale. Foster tried several times to broker a deal, but she wasn't going for it.

Hawkins then took over the sales pitch, visiting her often to see if she was ready to sell. She always gave the same answer—no.

Finally, in September of 1966, after Disney's project was announced, Mrs. Eassey decided to sell. She wanted to use the money from the sale to finance her son's education.

She too had a caveat to her land deal: she wanted a lifetime pass to Disneyland and Walt Disney World. Of course, the company obliged.[35]

These individual purchases were pretty straightforward. There were obviously certain challenges in tracking down the owners, but once that hurdle was cleared, the owners usually opted to sell.

When it was all said and done, after a year-and-a-half-long process, about sixty-five of the smaller properties had been purchased at an average price of about $350 an acre.[36]

With the major pieces of property under Disney's ownership and the acquisition of the hodgepodge of smaller lots, Walt had over 16,000 acres at his disposal. Today, these parcels make up the Magic Kingdom, Epcot, and Hollywood Studios resort area.[37]

If you recall, Walt initially—yet somewhat arbitrarily—decided he needed 5,000 to 10,000 acres for the project. He got his wish and then some.

However, he wasn't satisfied and wanted more—much more. Roy balked and told his kid brother they had enough. Walt immediately shot back, asking Roy if he wouldn't love to own another 5,000 acres around Disneyland now.[38]

Walt wanted more land, so Walt got more land. Foster, Helliwell, and Hawkins went after the previously mentioned Bronson property.

Another large parcel, this tract was about 8,000 acres. Interstate 4 divided the land, with a quarter of the acreage on the west side and three quarters on the east.[39]

Bonnet Creek, Reedy Creek, and the Reedy Creek Swamp crossed part of the property. Since it was across from the Demetree tract, the group working back in Burbank was already thinking ahead about water control from one property to another.

Should they need to do something with excess water, this property could be valuable. Engineers could run the drainage of the Demetree tract through the Bronson property and into Bonnet Creek, Reedy Creek, and the swamp.[40]

Looking even further down the pipeline, the Bronson property was in Osceola County, whereas the other tracts were in Orange County.[41] By straddling the two counties, if one county were to resist Disney's plans, the company could use their leverage and threaten to utilize the land in the other county.

These intangibles made it a great option to have and solidified the desire to acquire Bronson's property.

You heard the name Irlo Bronson Sr. once already in this book—today you can still hear it, as a large stretch of highway near the Disney property bears his name. Not only was Bronson a state senator and a fourth-generation cattle rancher, but he was also a big landowner (recall that he was the one who had sold the Demetree tract to the Demetree brothers and Jenkins in the first place).

Bronson used his parcel as a cow pasture, and he truthfully didn't need to sell his land, as he was quite well off. In fact, when questioned about how much land he owned in the area he confessed that he didn't actually know the exact number.[42]

Hawkins was tasked with acquiring the land from Bronson, as the two men knew each other. Hawkins stopped by his house one day to inquire about the property in question.

Bronson told him that he had a handshake deal to sell a local veterinarian the smaller parcel on the west side of Interstate 4.

Disappointed, Hawkins mentioned to Bronson that he would buy both pieces of the property, and he implored Bronson not to sell the larger parcel without contacting him first. Perhaps, Hawkins said, Bronson could even circle back to the veterinarian and see if he was still a buyer. If he wasn't, Hawkins would take it.

In August of 1964, Hawkins received a call from Bronson. He was optimistic that Bronson was calling to tell him Disney could purchase the property. That optimism quickly faded.

The state of Florida reached out to Bronson to tell him his land was going to be acquired at forty-five dollars an acre. It would be preserved and possibly used for a park or conservation.

The deal was going to happen fast too. The state had until the end of the year to acquire it or they would lose matching funds the federal government was offering to help the state purchase it.

Not only was the land being taken from him—and at a rate half of what Disney was willing to pay—but the whole scenario was totally disrespectful to him as a state senator.

Bronson couldn't believe his fellow Democratic lawmakers wanted to do this—each and every one of them knew the land was his. They also knew it was highly desirable. Still, they went ahead and expedited the process so the government could get the land as soon as possible. Bronson was fuming.

Hawkins got off the phone with Bronson and called down to Helliwell in Miami to relay the bad news. It was time for Helliwell to activate his network of good ol' boys once again.

Apparently, the department leading the charge to take Bronson's land was the Outdoor Recreational Council.

An influential member of that council was a man by the name of Broward Williams. He had also done a stint on the Board of Directors of the Florida Association of Insurance Companies.[43]

Can you take a guess as to who knew Mr. Williams? Yep, the ever-connected, insurance-company-owning, man about town, Paul Helliwell.

Helliwell told Williams that he was involved in a project that would change the face of Florida and this parcel was key. He couldn't speak more about it due to confidentiality issues, but Williams would have to trust him.

Needless to say, the state stopped moving in on the senator's property. Two weeks later Bronson sold his property to Disney, including the land that was originally being sold to the veterinarian. The sale price was just over $100 an acre.[44]

Walt, Roy, and their collection of sly proxies had done it. By late spring of 1965 they had purchased over forty-three square miles—equal to the size of San Francisco and roughly twice the size of Manhattan—for about $5 million. The average price per acre was under $200.

When looking back on his work, Foster was proud of what he had accomplished with Paul Helliwell and Roy Hawkins. He had fulfilled Roy's orders to buy the property at the right price, and under the right terms, so it could be justified as a proper investment for a public company.

As for Walt's expectations, he had fulfilled those too. He wouldn't have any other businesses encroaching on his dreams, as they had at Disneyland.

Walt now had a huge buffer of land for the project, which was a blank slate. There were no roads, powerlines, or sewer systems in place. He would be able to make this uninhabited paradise all his own.

The acquisition group had done a great job keeping the project a secret thus far, but they still weren't finished buying a few smaller adjacent parcels, nor were they ready to announce their intentions.

Secrecy would continue to be imperative—but pressure from the local newspapers was starting to ratchet up.

Chapter 6

NEVER A DULL MOMENT

As we've read, the logistics of Disney's acquisition plan had Foster, Helliwell, and Hawkins, either separately or all together, negotiate the land deals. Once the terms were finalized, the purchases were placed in Helliwell's name as a trustee—the transactions were made in cash to make it a bit more difficult to trace them back to Walt and Roy.

Like all real estate transactions, these properties were deeded and titled with the county. Since such information is a matter of public record—and often appeared in local newspapers' legal notice sections in those days—utilizing Helliwell as the trustee and shell corporations as the owner provided an extra layer of anonymity for Disney.

Let's read about some of the specifics of the shell corporations from a meeting on Tuesday, June 15, 1965, at 10:00 a.m., in Conference Room 2E, at the Disney studio in Burbank, California:

> *Bob Foster opened the meeting with a statement that we had invested $183 per acre in our Florida project as compared with approximately $3,500 per acre at Disneyland. Property in Anaheim is now selling at $97,000 an acre.*
>
> *Bob outlined that the property had been acquired by five Florida corporations: Reedy Creek Ranch, Inc., Bay Lake Properties, Inc., Tomahawk Properties, Inc., Aye Four Corporation and Latin American Development and Management Corporation.*
>
> *All of the stock of each of the forgoing corporations is owned by Compass East Corporation, a Delaware corporation. Each of*

the forgoing corporations has an authorized capitalization of $25,000 consisting of 25,000 shares of $1 par value, [and] is on a fiscal year ending September 30.

Aside from an initial capital contribution to each of the Florida corporations of $1,250, the balance of the purchase price of the land which they acquired has been advanced by Compass East Corporation, which in turn has borrowed the money from Walt Disney Productions.

No notes have yet been drawn nor have financial records other than cash accounts been prepared. The practice has been for Reedy Creek Ranch Inc., to pay all of the expenses (for which it is entitled to reimbursement) and that corporation also owns the Bronson home and surrounding property.[1]

As noted, this meeting was in mid-June of '65. Down in Orlando at that time, the rumor mill about these deals had already started to churn.

The month before this corporate meeting, the central Florida newspapers had started to report on the project, as real estate paperwork had been filed at the county level.

Here are the very first mentions of the real estate transactions in the Orlando newspapers. These covered the first four major purchases (Bronson, Bay Lake, Demetree, and Hamrick).

The first appearance was in the May 4, 1965, edition of the *Orlando Sentinel*. The headline read "Huge Tract Completed: 1.5 Million Paid In Big Land Deal":

Kissimmee—two large real estate transactions, totaling almost $1.5 million, were recorded in the office of Glenn Ray, Osceola Land Clerk. The larger sale, involving 8,380 acres of land, was made by Bronsons Inc., of Kissimmee, to Latin-American

ORIGINAL LAND PURCHASES
BY SHELL COMPANY NAME

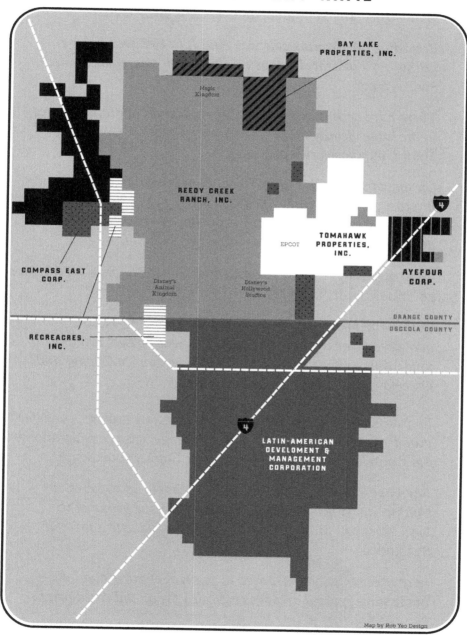

Map by Rob Yeo Design

Development and Management Corp., whose address was given as 600 Brickell Ave., Miami. According to stamps on the deed, the selling price was $900,000, an average of $107 an acre.

Recording the Bronson sale was Paul L.E. Helliwell, whose calling card indicated he has offices both in Miami and Zurich, Switzerland.

There have been two other smaller recordings of property sales in the same vicinity recently. Reedy Creek Ranch Corp., also of Miami, purchased two parcels.

Closing of sale on this large tract of land will, undoubtedly, increase rumors already afloat for the last year, to the effect that a new and large industrial complex is about to locate to the area.[2]

On May 20, 1965, the *Orlando Sentinel* headline was "Two More Large Tracts Sold: New Facility To Provide 5000 Jobs":

Two more links in the chain of title to a growing 25,000-acre development which will, within a year or two, bring an unidentified industry employing 5,000 persons to Orange and Osceola counties were forged Wednesday.

Florida Ranch Lands, Inc. Orlando real estate brokers, confirmed that deeds to two parcels of land involving a cash consideration of $285,000 had been filed in the Orange County courthouse.

Bay Lake Properties, Inc., Miami, purchased 1,250 acres in southwest Orange from Bay Isles Associates, a group of 10 local investors. Stamps affixed to the deed indicate a price of $250,000.

In another transaction a deed to 55 acres of grove and land in the same general area was recorded for an indicated price *of $35,000. Sellers were Jerry and Lillian Ross; purchasers, Reedy Creek Ranch Inc., Miami.*

To date, the cash purchases of thousands of acres of land in the same general area total between $2.5 and $3 million.

Although rumors concerning use of the large acreage have been wild and numerous, the purchasers—and its ultimate use— have never been officially identified.

There has been one constant rumor that the land is being purchased for a second east coast Disneyland attraction, but little credence is given this in view of the fact that Walt Disney himself, in a recent statement to the Orlando Sentinel *while on a visit to Cape Kennedy, said he was spending $50 million to expand his California attraction and had neither the time nor the talent to look for a second venture. In short, Mr. Disney said he already had his hands full.*[3]

May 26, 1965, the *Evening Star* front-page headline stated "Mystery Industry Options $2.3 Million More Land":

Options on the two remaining large tracts of land in the 'mystery industry' area in southwest Orange County and Osceola County were claimed today to the tune of $2.3 million. Money has been sent to exercise options on some 12,500 acres owned by Jack and Bill Demetree and Bill Jenkins, as well as 2,650 acres owned by Wilson and Carroll Hamrick of Apopka. A spokesman for Florida Lands Inc., confirmed this morning.[4]

One last headline and blurb from May 28, 1965, from the *Evening Star*—"Mystery Buying Tops $5 Million":

Cash land purchases by the unidentified company which plans to construct a plant employing 5,000 persons near Orlando *have exceeded the staggering sum of $5 million. To be exact: $5,018,770.*

This became clear today when Florida Ranch Lands, Inc., Orlando broker, supplied the Evening Star with a detailed breakdown of 47 transactions made by it for the unidentified buyer.

What the new industry will be, no one knows except the buyers and they aren't telling.[5]

According to the *Evening Star,* nobody was certain which industry was coming to town. It wasn't Walt Disney, because he said so, and Uncle Walt wouldn't lie to us—or would he?

So, it was back to rumor mill, which included just about anyone and everyone. The default was that a manufacturing plant was coming to town, which made sense for the time and location.

Basically all of the aviation companies were rumored as possible candidates too. Howard Hughes, with one of his corporations, was probably coming to town, people said, or if not Hughes, then definitely Douglas Aviation, Lockheed, or McDonnell Aircraft.

Next up were the car companies. Ford, Chrysler, and Volkswagen were all solid contenders at some point according to word on the street.

There were even rumors that a Rockefeller was coming, due to David Rockefeller having a loose affiliation with a professor at Rollins College.[6]

Folks were even writing the papers with tips from their mothers' uncles' second cousins twice removed from South Dakota who heard from their barbers that it was definitely someone in aviation since the land was close to the space coast.

Long before the days of the Internet and social media, our society was very newspaper-centric and -driven. For a small town like Orlando to have someone gobble up roughly 25,000 acres and spend over $5 million, it was quite a big deal.

The local papers, most notably the *Orlando Sentinel*, closely covered the story and consistently kept the rumors in play.

At the very least, there was a weekly story every Sunday that published the names of the parties involved in the land deals filed for the week.

There was another column at the *Sentinel* called "Hush Puppies," written by Charlie Wadsworth. Mr. Wadsworth frequently reported about the dealings. He often made fun of, or light of, the guesses being thrown about town.

Helliwell and Hawkins dabbled in the arena of gossip too. They added to the speculation and flagrantly joked about it, almost taunting those who hung on every rumor.

At the Florida Bankers Association conference in '65, Helliwell admitted toward the end of his speech that word had finally leaked out regarding all of the property in his name. He wanted to confirm that it was, in fact . . . the Ford Motor Company. They needed all of that land for their Mustangs.[7] (A little tongue in cheek there by Helliwell.)

Hawkins got in on the hearsay as well. On a quick vacation to Seattle, home to Boeing, he purchased a few postcards featuring the aerospace company's plant. Before he left town, he mailed them back to central Florida, hoping to keep the mystery alive.[8]

While it was fun for Helliwell and Hawkins to stoke the fire, the truth was, as the summer of 1965 soldiered on, the stories were bringing a lot of attention to the project. The pressure was really starting to mount for everyone involved.

Helliwell, Hawkins, and Foster really wanted to get a break from the constant attention and speculation. They looked again to utilize their connections to see if they could get some respite.

This scheme brought two big-time Florida powerbrokers together, one from the southern part of the state and the other from the middle; Paul Helliwell, meet Billy Dial.

Dial was an attorney (naturally, who isn't in these stories!) but not just any attorney. At times, he represented the city of Orlando, the *Orlando Sentinel*, the biggest bank in town, and some of the area's largest employers, including Martin Marietta and CSX Railways.[9]

Dial knew all of the movers and shakers in central Florida, one of which was his friend Martin Andersen—the owner and publisher of the *Orlando Sentinel*.

According to legend and lore, Helliwell, by way of Dial, persuaded Andersen to take a break from the front-page news and stream of stories about the land acquisitions.

There is some ambiguity and mystery to this storyline. We know the men met, but we don't know what, if anything, transpired between them.

Dial went on the record during an interview with *Orlando-Land* magazine:

> *The problem was that they had some pieces of property that they had not been able to secure—what we call 'ins.' They were inside of the parameters of the general property. One was a piece of grove property. They said they couldn't afford any leaks as to who this was until they could get all of their ducks in row.*
>
> *Well, I took them down and introduced them to Mr. (Martin) Andersen, who was then publisher of the paper, and he agreed to cooperate by not publishing any iffy stories, that type of thing. We knew that first time we recorded some deeds, the fat would be in the fire. Everyone would be looking and guessing who it was.*[10]

Andersen, on the other hand, was adamant that he hadn't known Disney had been behind the deals, nor had he protected the company or betrayed his journalistic integrity by not accurately and honestly reporting about such a huge story in town.

In 1977 Andersen went on record and repeated that he had met Helliwell, and had known he was attached to a large land deal, but "never did Helliwell, Dial or anyone else ever tell me it was a Disney project. And never did I ask."[11]

Since the men are long deceased, we will probably never know the truth. However, there was a third party who may have had some proof that Andersen had cooperated a bit with Helliwell. Her name was Emily Bavar.

Ms. Bavar was a writer for *Florida* magazine and the *Orlando Sentinel*. On a press junket to the Disney studios, along with five other journalists, for the tenth anniversary celebration of Disneyland, she spoke directly to Walt.

Disney had flown the journalists out on their plane, given them a tour of Disneyland and the studio, and then provided them with access to Walt.

In turn, the journalists wrote stories about Disney in their local papers. This was a common marketing and advertising thing Disney did back in the day.

Ms. Bavar, like the other journalists, wrote a story about Disney in her paper—just not the story Walt wanted.

When she had her opportunity to question Walt—about anything—Bavar asked a pretty benign and straightforward question: Are you buying all of that land in Orlando?

Walt had often fielded this question over the prior few months. He normally gave a very basic "no" or said, "I'm too busy with other things," or something in that vain.

This time it seemed as though Walt was either caught off guard by Bavar's question, overthought his answer, or both. He ended up tipping his hand to her. Walt rambled on too much, at least in Bavar's opinion. Here's Walt's reply to her simple question:

I've heard those rumors and reports from Florida . . . I have studied Florida. I visited all the big attractions. I wanted to see how they did things and how they handled the crowds. You have some beautiful spots in Florida. I've seen them. But you have some problems.[12]

Walt proceeded to talk about those problems and then, for some reason, babbled on about how he could actually remedy them.

Well, that was all Bavar needed to hear. Walt didn't adamantly or boldly deny it once and for all. Even a mere "no" could have sufficed. Instead, he just kept talking.

After her exchange with Walt, Bavar's instincts told her Disney was, in fact, the company behind the land deals. She sent a story back to her editor and Andersen.

She told them about her conversation with Walt and that she was absolutely sure it was Disney coming to town. That story made it into the *Sentinel* on October 16, buried on page twenty-three.[13]

Disappointed with where her story landed, Bavar, once she was back in Florida, met with Andersen. She gave him more details and was unwavering that Disney was the "mystery industry."

Andersen and other editors at the paper apologized for not taking her story more seriously.[14] On October 21, 1965, the front-page headline of the *Sentinel* read "Is Our 'Mystery' Industry Disneyland?"

Three days later, the *Orlando Sentinel* ran another front-page headline. This time they weren't asking if Disney was the mystery industry, the were proclaiming it: "We Say: 'Mystery' Industry Is Disney"

As history shows, Emily Bavar was correct, and she figured out Disney's secret over a month before the company was going to announce its plans.[15]

Looks like we will never know if the October 16 story was deliberately buried or not. What we do know is folks around Walt were nervous for him during the press junket in which Bavar had participated.

Foster happened to be at the encounter between Walt and Bavar. As he recounted years later:

What Ms. Bavar didn't know was that several of us sat at the "lawyers" table across the dining room from Walt's table on that fateful day. We watched and speculated on who in the party was from the Orlando Sentinel, and when the damaging questions would be asked and how Walt was going to answer.[16]

So how did Walt, Roy, and the rest of the group hear about the printed headline, and how did they react to it?

When the story graced the front page, Foster and a few other Disney executives were staying at the Robert Meyer Motor Inn in Orlando. Ironically, they were in town scouting out a location to hold the November announcement for the project.

As Foster stepped off of the elevator that Sunday morning to grab breakfast, he was met by General Joe Potter—more on Joe in chapter eight—who had a copy of the paper in his hands.[17]

Seeing that it was 8:00 a.m. on the East Coast, it was too early to call California and inform Walt and Roy. Truth be told, no one wanted to be the one to break the news to the brothers anyway.

Foster called to Helliwell down in Miami and let him know the situation. The decision was made to call Disney executive Card Walker in California and have him tell the Disneys.

The brothers took the news as best they could. Rather than deny it again, they embraced and accepted it. Still, this early announcement did cost Disney a bit of money, and possibly a few opportunities.

Foster was looking to fill in the gaps around the property. They still needed to buy several hundred acres. The day after the headline hit, land prices in the area skyrocketed to over $1,000 an acre.

Even with Disney willing to pay the higher prices, as the saying goes, "there's always one that gets away." In Disney's case, it was more than one.

One such piece of land is called Bonnet Creek. If you drive around the Disney property, you may see signs for it. The parcel wasn't developed until 2004 when several hotels were built, most notably the Waldorf Astoria.

These 480 acres are surrounded by Disney on three sides, and the fourth side backs up to Interstate 4.

The owner of the property randomly speculated on the land back in 1962. Seeing that it wasn't too far from the space coast, and adjacent to major thoroughfares, they figured it could be used for warehouses or something industrial.

Foster and Hawkins tried for months to get in touch with the owner in Asia. Once they were in contact with an intermediary, they were informed that the owner wasn't interested in selling. Disney went ahead and built around the property.

Another property that Disney failed to acquire was owned by cattle rancher Oren Brown. Disney reportedly offered him $4.2 million for his 6,750 acres and his portion of the Reedy Creek Swamp.

Brown wasn't interested in selling; he was quoted in 1971, saying, "What's money? It's only paper, most of it . . . I never could keep money. The land, it won't run off. Lots of people like money, but I don't care so much for it. I reckon I'm peculiar that way."[18]

Some fifty years later, Disney finally got its land when, in 2019, the company purchased over 1,600 acres from Brown's family for roughly $11 million.[19]

From L-R General William Potter, Robert P. Foster, Roy H. Hawkins, Paul Helliwell, Richard Morrow, Governor Hayden Burns October 25, 1965

But let's get back to that day in 1965. By the evening, Foster, General Potter, and the rest of the group at the Robert Meyer Motor Inn headed down to Miami to meet up with Helliwell. Once in Miami, Foster placed a call to Florida's Governor, Haydon Burns, to confirm the news the *Sentinel* broke.[20]

It turned out the governor was set to be in Miami the next morning to address the annual convention of the League of Municipalities. Disney's executives met the governor the next morning on his plane. They brought him up to date on the project.[21]

Governor Burns asked for them to be his guests at the convention. He wanted a Disney presence there since he was going to close out his appearance by confirming the company was coming to Florida.

As promised, Burns proclaimed that Disney was bringing "the greatest attraction yet known in the history of Florida" and "this was the most important event in Florida history."[22]

The governor was rightfully excited; this was a big win, not only for the state, but hopefully for him as well.

It was an election year, and Burns was running against the Mayor of Miami, Bob High. This announcement was quite the coup for the governor—he was able to announce the project in his opponent's hometown.

Burns really wanted to glom onto Disney as best he could. He even went so far as to claim he had been a consultant on the project from its beginning. The media was quick to question him on that.[23]

Immediately after the big announcement Burns made a call to Walt Disney to congratulate him. The two agreed that November 15, 1965, would be the date for the official press conference.

The governor was so excited to welcome Walt to the state. He even pushed hard to get him a ticker tape parade through town on the day of the press conference.

A parade was something Walt would absolutely not do (which is interesting considering his history with parades both inside and outside of Disneyland). Walt urged those working closely around him to get the governor off of his back—there would be no parade.[24]

After the announcement, Disney wasted no time in getting started on its land and preparing for the company's first official appearance in Florida, slated for November 15.

On October 29, 1965, the *Orlando Sentinel* ran a story detailing some movement on the Disney property. They had started experimental land clearing:

Edwards Construction Co. of Indiantown, Florida has already cleared a 300-acre plot on the northwest corner of Interstate 4's connection with Florida 530.

Engineers of the firm Gee and Jensen, consulting engineers of West Palm Beach, have already launched water control, hydraulics and drainage studies on the property.[25]

You can surmise that, back in the boardroom, the team was working hard as well. They needed to come up with a master plan, along with some possible concessions from the state and county, for a project of this magnitude.

Until now, all anyone really knew was that Disney was coming to town. No one outside Disney knew exactly what was in store for the site. Perhaps the press conference would put an end to the mystery—or perhaps it would only add to it.

The November 15 press conference was held in the Egyptian Room of the Cherry Plaza Hotel in Orlando. Walt and Roy started off that day aboard their corporate Gulfstream. Flying at a low altitude, they saw their property for the first time from the air.[26]

By the afternoon, the brothers were in front of the media, both local and national. With the governor by their side, they spoke in general terms about the project and fielded questions from the audience.

Not a whole lot of details were released that day, despite the buildup of anticipation. Walt seemed pretty vague, not willing to commit to specifics, time frames, or financial expenditures.

November 15, 1965, The Florida Memory Project.

He did speak broadly about needing some control over the land so he wouldn't make the same mistakes he had at Disneyland. Here are Walt's first public comments about the project from the press conference (when Governor Burns introduced him, Walt's midwestern farm boy charm kicked in):

Well Mr. Governor, it's been a wonderful reception that you've given us here . . . All the faces seem friendly, and we feel very much at home. And, of course this is a big exciting project for us too.

You know, I mean, in fact it's the biggest thing we've ever tackled, and I might for the benefit of the press, explain that my brother and I have been together in our business for forty-two years now.

He's my big brother and he's the one that when I was a little fellow I used to go to with some of my wild ideas and he'd either straighten me out and put me on the right path or something, or if he didn't agree with me I'd work on it for years until I got him to agree with me.

But I must say that we've had our problems that way and that's been the proper balance that we've been needing in our organization. And he watches out for the financial side of it, the corporate side and in this project though I'd like to say that I didn't have to work very hard with him on this project.

He was with me from the start. Now whether that's good or bad, I don't know [Walt laughs].

But I think that to have this enthusiasm on the part of our whole organization and on the part of the people of the state of Florida really is a good start.

And we hope that what we develop here will be a real credit to the state, a credit to the Disney organization and I might say that when we were planning Disneyland, and we hoped that we could build something that would command the respect of the community.

And after ten years I feel that we've accomplished that . . . not only the community but the country as a whole. And that is actually what we hope to do here . . . is to really develop something that, ah, oh, just more than an entertainment enterprise . . . it's something that contributes in many other ways . . . ah.

Well, educationally, and the one thing to me . . . the important thing . . . is the family, and if you can keep the family together with things . . . and that's been the backbone of our whole business, catering to the families and that's what we hope to do.[27]

After Walt's opening remarks, the governor spoke, and then both he and Walt fielded a few questions, mostly centering around if this project was going to be another Disneyland.

Walt readily admitted that he had a lot of ideas, but they weren't ready to be shared with the public. His first public appearance as a new landowner in Florida was largely uneventful, as he divulged very little new information.

There was one question however that did seem to pique his interest, and he went into a bit more detail when compared with the answers to the other questions: Will you have a model community to take care of the aggregation of people?

Well, those are the things we have to analyze. You see, this comes into . . . this comes into this initial state of getting all those things brought together and setting up a plan for the whole complex.

And we have done a lot of thinking on a model community and I would like to be a part of building a model community, a city of tomorrow as you might say, because I don't believe in going out to this extreme blue sky stuff that some of the architects do.

I believe people still want, want to live like human beings. But still there's a lot that could be done. I'm not against the automobile but I just feel that the automobile had moved into communities too, too much and I feel that you can design so that the automobile is there but still put people back as pedestrians again, you see.

So I don't know, I'd love to work on a project like that. Also, I mean, in the way of schools, facilities for the community, well, community entertainments and life. I'd love to be a part of building up a school of tomorrow with the teaching age with what I feel we could contribute, which we had been doing in a way. But this might become a pilot operation for the teaching age. But to go out across the country and across the world. The great problem today is the one of teaching.[28]

An interesting blurb and window into what he was truly thinking about for this project.

Even though it wasn't disclosed at this press conference, the reality was Walt had a pretty exacting plan in mind, not just an abundance of ideas.

His new project had evolved and superseded the disappointment and limitations he saw at Disneyland.

Walt intended to reinvent, or remanufacture, the way in which we lived, worked, and played as a society and community. He called it Progress City.

He still faced a long list of logistics and details to work through, most notably the control over his land, even though at the press conference it didn't seem like there was much to worry about there—Burns had basically conceded and said he was willing to fully cooperate with whatever Disney wanted.

L-R: Roy Disney, Governor Haydon Burns, Mrs. Burns, Walt Disney. November 15, 1965.
The Florida Memory Project.

Unfortunately, for those in attendance, and for the public in general, they would have to wait, yet again, for the big reveal from Disney regarding what it would bring to central Florida.

After the press conference, the Disney executives were the guests of honor at a reception featuring the governor and a who's who of key players in Florida—Walt and Roy even had the pleasure of meeting Martin Andersen from the *Orlando Sentinel.*

The next day, the brothers got the official on-the-ground tour of their property. In his own unique way, without overtly showing it, Walt loved what he saw.

He boated across Bay Lake and had a picnic (he had requested southern fried chicken for lunch) at the old Bronson house—today this spot is part of Disney's Saratoga Springs resort.[29]

Walt, Roy, and the entire group headed back to California. On the flight back, attorney Dick Morrow questioned Walt about his thoughts regarding the state's involvement with his land and their cooperation with his plans.

Helliwell and the group, along with the Donovan law firm, advocated that the only solution for Walt would be to have his own municipality.[30]

Morrow was curious if Walt had ever given much thought to the scenario. Walt informed him he was not in favor of it at all. He remarked that he had shared some information with Jules Stein, who was the head of Universal Studios, and he had told him not to allow his project to become a municipality.

Stein's Universal Tours project had been incorporated as a municipality—Universal City—which was surrounded by Los Angeles. He claimed it was a nightmare dealing with the city and the County of Los Angeles.

Morrow shot back and told Walt not to listen to Stein—the municipality was the only way to go.[31]

Walt's temper flared; he didn't like what he was hearing from Morrow, who at that point decided it was best to leave the subject alone and take up the fight at a later date.

Regardless of this disagreement, the trip and the press conference were a huge success. The Disney brothers were happy with how everything had worked out, despite the announcement not initially being on their terms.

History shows that central Florida—and arguably the entire state—was never the same after that press conference. As one member of the media remarked at the time: "Walt would be the most celebrated visitor since Ponce De León."[32]

As for Foster, Helliwell, Hawkins, and the rest of the crew, they were able to keep everything a secret for about eighteen months, which was a pretty good run. In some respects, their work was coming to an end, but in others, it was just beginning.

Chapter 7

HORIZONS

Walt was highly proficient at making something from nothing. He had made a career out of it. However, the scope and magnitude of this project was quite an undertaking, even for him.

Not to mention he was hovering around the point in life when many people his age start to collect Social Security and move down to Florida—at least he got that part right.

Judging by the few morsels of information gleaned from the press conference in November of 1965, Walt wanted to explore building a city of tomorrow.

The man who created the world's most famous mouse and revolutionized family entertainment across many verticals was set to become an urban planner.

Much of Walt's adult life was spent in the eyes of the media. He sat for thousands of interviews and offered up hundreds of noteworthy quotes, many of which still linger on today.

Probably the one quote he was most proud of (and the Walt Disney Company still utilizes) wasn't said by the man himself. It wasn't even directly about him, but about something he had conceived: "I may hold a view that may be somewhat shocking to an audience as sophisticated as this, that the greatest piece of urban design in the United States today is Disneyland."

This quote came from James Rouse, an urban planner and real estate developer who brought malls and planned communities to the East Coast.

At the 1963 Urban Design Conference at Harvard University, Rouse was the keynote speaker, and he delivered a speech that lauded Walt's Disneyland. Here's more of the quote:

I may hold a view that may be somewhat shocking to an audience as sophisticated as this, that the greatest piece of urban design in the United States today is Disneyland . . . It took an area of activity—the amusement park—and lifted it to a standard so high in performance, in its respect for people, in its functioning for people, that it really does become a brand new thing. It fulfills all its functions it set out to accomplish— unselfconsciously, usefully and profitably to its owners and developers. I find more to learn in the standards that have been set and in the goals that have been achieved in the development of Disneyland than in any other piece of physical development in the country.[1]

Walt loved this quote, despite some of his personal misgivings on the subject. As discussed earlier in this book, one of the catalysts for Walt's desire to develop this project was the issues that had popped up at Disneyland: the encroaching chaos, commercialization, and urbanization that he considered a blight to his magic kingdom.

As he looked across the country, he realized this wasn't just a problem for him at Disneyland; he saw how urbanization was affecting and changing the United States.

Walt briefly mentioned something during his November press conference about how the automobile was a game changer. He didn't necessarily think it was a good thing in terms of society and urban sprawl.

As a young child, Walt's father moved his family from the urban life of Chicago to the farm life of Marceline, Missouri. It had more of a relaxed, controlled environment compared to Chicago.

Walt's time spent on this farm, albeit only a few short years, impacted his life more so than any other period of his upbringing. He loved the rural, small town setting. As an adult, he longed for and romanticized this era.

Visitors to Disneyland see this almost immediately upon entering. Main Street—which looks like most any town in the USA at the turn of the twentieth century—greets guests as they transition from the real world into Walt's world. Escapes to another time and place from the past are also seen in Frontierland and Adventureland.

A similar yet different scene is set in Tomorrowland, which sends visitors into the future. Next is Fantasyland, where visitors are only bound by their timeless imaginations.

If it is possible for one to wax nostalgic, yet also be a futurist, that person was Walt Disney. As his Disneyland illustrates, he was not only influenced by the past but the future—and the improbable.

Walt believed he could meld a few of these concepts together and create a new city. It would feature the latest technology yet be rooted in the ideals and sense of an organic community happiness from yesterday.

Technology would simplify life in some respects and advance them in others. You would live, work, and play in a centralized community. The city would be engineered to be simplistic, symbiotic, and regulated on many levels—with no bustling commute, traffic or rat race.

The automobile wouldn't be necessary either. In Walt's city, you would catch a lift on the WEDway PeopleMover, as seen in Disneyland during the 1960s.

This optimal way to travel around town would take you to your home, your job, and anywhere else you could ever want or need to go. The majority of your shopping would be done on your Main Street—or something that resembled it in concept, such as a futuristic shopping hub.

Since Walt had been able to successfully manufacture his utopia known as Disneyland, which allowed visitors to leave today and enter the world of yesterday, tomorrow, and fantasy (as the plaque at the entrance to his park states), he figured he could probably do the same thing for people in their day-to-day lives.

Interestingly, though, Walt didn't necessarily want to try to fix the existing way in which we lived. He wanted to recreate it, starting from scratch, with his new concept. At its core, this became his Florida project and his final dream.

There would be no better way for Walt to convey his ideas and dreams to the public than by making a film about them. Ever the showman, he was no stranger to working as an on-screen pitchman. (I've often surmised that Walt was the creator of the first infomercial.)

In 1954 and part of 1955, leading up to the opening of Disneyland, the television show *Walt Disney's Disneyland* gave viewers a coming attraction of what they would find when they visited his theme park.

Through the show, viewers could watch the park transform in front of their eyes, without ever leaving their homes.

They became familiar with the layout and themes, as Walt produced stories that mimicked the geography of the park, including Frontierland, Adventureland, Fantasyland, and so forth.

Walt's sly infomercial about the Disneyland project masqueraded as an entertaining television program to garner interest in his new endeavor; it was quite savvy.

Millions of viewers across the country tuned in each week. They made the television show a smash hit and contributed to the successful launch of the theme park.

The situation in Florida was similar. Walt needed to "sell" his ideas to an audience. This time it was the state of Florida, both its population and legislature.

However, the repercussions, and whether or not the project failed or succeeded, wouldn't just impact his company—this situation would influence and affect the entire state of Florida.

Absolute legal control of the property was on the line. Disney wanted Florida to grant governmental powers to a company in the private sector, which seemed extremely risky for the state.

Walt was once asked why he didn't run for office. His response was, "Why be a governor or a senator when you can be king of

Disneyland?"[2] The way things were shaping up in Florida, it was starting to look like he could become all three.

Before Disney World could come to life, he needed to further creatively, and legally, define and refine it. His trusted group of attorneys who assembled his land deals were hard at work outlining their wants and needs from, and possible concessions to, the county and state.

As the existing state legislation stood, the Disney think tank envisioned problems with making their project work. It seemed as though 1966 was going to be a year of preparation for both the legal and physical landscape of the property, as problems were also afoot on site in Florida.

It appeared as though the majority of Disney's land spent much of its time under water. Initial surveys revealed roughly 75 percent of the property could be under water during the summer season.[3]

The Gee & Jensen engineering group was brought in to examine the situation. As a Florida corporation, its engineers were familiar with the lay of the land, both literally and technically. They knew how Disney should handle the situation.[4]

According to Florida Statute Chapter 298, Disney could form a drainage district. This would allow them to control and move the excess water around their property via canals, levees, bridges, and things of that nature.[5]

Equally, if not more importantly to Disney, especially from Roy's point of view, these districts could sell bonds to fund that work.[6]

No legislation was needed to form the district. It could be formed via district court. If Disney jumped through the appropriate legal hoops, its district would be created without a problem.

In May of 1966, the aptly named Reedy Creek Drainage District was approved—as discussed, the actual Reedy Creek runs through a large portion of Disney's property.

This district authorized Disney to control its land reclamation project without government interference. This allowed Disney to make about 20,000 of their over 24,000 acres usable by dredging roughly fifty miles of canals.

When Walt caught a glimpse of the first canal created, he demanded that it be done again, as it was totally straight. He wanted his canals to look natural, to sort of meander with a curve and not have a man-made appearance.

The Reedy Creek Drainage District was Disney's first step toward having control over the property. As the drainage district came together, the legal group did its due diligence and made a rough outline of what it believed the project required.

Foremost, the group wanted legislation to protect Disney's intellectual property, trademarks, and tradenames so no one could knock off its merchandise and products. As it stood, the Florida statutes were not strong enough for Disney's needs.[7]

Next, Disney wanted the authority to construct, own, finance, and operate the following:

- Roads, bridges, and related structures, along with the power to connect them to public roads.
- Water, sewer, and public utility systems.
- An airport, transportation systems, and parking facilities.
- Mosquito and pest-control facilities and areas of conservation.
- Fire protection and waste collection and disposal services.
- A limited right of eminent domain, as provided in state statutes on drainage and water control systems.[8]

Disney also wanted the authority to exempt its land from state statutes, county ordinances, and regulations, with respect to land use, planning, zoning, or subdivision of land; from all safety, building, and construction codes; and from the jurisdiction and authority of the Florida Public Utilities Commission.[9]

Disney's power and authority would be limited to only within the land's boundaries, but the company would have the power and authority to exercise its functions within the boundaries of any city within this land.

The company also wanted the power to issue bonds and other financial securities to finance its activities and have the authority to levy taxes, and to impose liens to enforce unpaid taxes.[10]

Lastly, Disney wanted to create two municipal corporations: the City of Bay Lake and the City of Lake Buena Vista.[11]

Not asking for too much, right!? When Walt built Disneyland, a vastly smaller project, he asked the city of Anaheim to help with infrastructure and improvements to roads and water and sewer systems to the tune of $153,000 (which they did).[12] Walt would cover that expense in Florida, as Disney *merely* wanted sovereignty.

Roy was more than a little concerned with making these heavy demands on the state. He knew they needed protection and help, but what was considered reasonable?[13]

During a committee meeting at Disney headquarters, which included all of the committee members except Walt, Hawkins brought up a few examples of what the state of Florida had recently done for other businesses.

He noted that Pratt-Whitney got exactly what it wanted in terms of land, roads, and seclusion.

General Electric, in Daytona, had major requests for specific utility features for its property. The state fulfilled its needs.

Aerojet needed land, flood control measures, and the construction of a canal. The state satisfied this list to ensure the company would come and do business.[14]

Committee member General Joe Potter contributed to the meeting by saying the techniques and materials needed to construct Disney World—most notably new plastics for walls and roofs, along with Disney's voltage requirements for attractions and fountains—were probably unlike anything the state has used or seen before.

Since that was the case, it was reasonable for Disney to ask for its own building code standards. Helliwell chimed in and noted that, at the time, Osceola County didn't even have building or zoning ordinances in place.[15]

Tom DeWolf, Helliwell's law partner, took Helliwell's point one step further, highlighting Disney's newly formed drainage district:

Another special feature of the drainage district is the possibility of incorporating within it other public utility features such as water supply systems, sewage disposal systems, road and highway systems and power systems. There is some precedent in Florida for adding these additional powers to a drainage district and presumably we can go as far in this regard as the legislature is willing to go.[16]

Helliwell further expounded:

There were two methods to form a municipal corporation, under the general law (which they shouldn't do) and by special act of the state legislature. Under the special act procedure, the state adopts for the municipality a charter which is specifically prepared for the desired purpose and which prevails over all general laws except where specifically made subject to general laws. If a change in the charter subsequently becomes necessary, it is generally necessary to go back to the legislature except in those situations where provision is made for a public referendum.

The charter will set forth the type of municipal government and desired administration. The municipality would also be entitled to various county and state refunds.[17]

This would be the plan: have the state incorporate Disney's drainage district, add a city or two, make a few other legislative tweaks, and it could all be collectively called a "Super District." If Disney could pull this off, it had carte blanche authority over the land.

The next biggest hurdle the committee had was to do some convincing. Not to the state of Florida—not yet at least—but to Walt.

He was still stuck on the advice from Jules Stein about not having his project incorporated as a city.

Foster was tasked with explaining what the group came up with and pitching it to Walt. Let's read about the pitch directly from Foster:

To illustrate our problem to Walt I prepared a series of four by six-inch cards, each card bearing the word or words describing or identifying each of these functions that had to be vested in some entity if they were going to be performed.

Some were proprietary functions of a city or county and some dealt with civil matters. Those that were proprietary could be delegated to a private entity or an entity governed through freehold elections, such as the Super District.

Those matters dealing with civil matters or civil activities of individuals could not be so delegated; each of these matters was also represented by a four by six-inch card. I arranged the cards on the boardroom wall in a prearranged sequence beside a larger card marked Super District.

I also had a large card marked municipality that I did not display. It would appear later if things went as I hoped they would. After several rehearsals, satisfied that the presentation was at my convincing best I scheduled a meeting with Walt.

Ostensibly, the meeting was to explain the proposed Super District that would encompass the entire property. To avoid interruptions and irrelevant discussion that was typical of Disney meetings, I arranged that only Walt would attend the meeting and as support I asked Dick Morrow to join in. I wanted support if the discussion became controversial.

With my audience of two I deliberately spoke slowly, explaining each governmental function, what it involved, how it could be financed and how and why it could be performed by the district and then placing the card under the Super District.

When I completed the explanation of the district the cards displayed under Super District, it would show it's completely its authority organization and function.

Those cards that remained were the problems. They were all governmental functions dealing with civil matters and would have to either be performed by the entities now performing them whoever it might be and wherever it might be located; or they could be vested in a newly created municipality.

As I approached the end of the presentation, having all of the districts' authority explained and the cards representing municipality powers remaining, Walt fulfilled his reputation by commenting, "my god Bob you speak slowly, all of these left over will have to be put in a city."

The log jam had been broken; I could display the "Municipality" card. It was then and there that the "golden spike was driven" closing the gap for the creation of the governmental structure for Project X.[18]

A few weeks after Foster gave his talk, he was summoned for a meeting with Walt. It was now Walt providing a presentation.[19]

The gentlemen took a seat in a studio projection room and viewed what Walt had been working on—the plan for the Florida.

Known today as the "E.P.C.O.T. film," back then it was loosely termed the "Florida film" or "Florida Project film" or "Walt's Florida film."

Walt started work on it in early 1966 and kept it secret, even from much of the group closest to him. Production of the film wrapped in one day, October 27, 1966.[20]

This film brought everything together, featuring many of the innovations Walt had developed and the lessons he had learned over his four decades in business and six decades of life—this was Walt's magnum opus, or so he hoped.

As Walt stood in front of the camera—the set strewn with maps, props, and models—he finally let the world into his future world down in Florida. Here's what he had to say:

Welcome to a little bit of Florida here in California. This is where the early planning is taking place for our so-called Disney World project. Now the purpose of this film is to bring you up to date about some of the plans for Disney World. But before I go into any of the details, I want to say just a word about the site for our Florida project.

As you can see on this map, we have a perfect location in Florida, almost in the very center of the state. In fact, we've selected this site because it's so easy for tourists and Florida residents to get here by automobile.

Now in larger scale on this map, our Florida land is located partly in Orange County and Osceola County between the cities of Orlando and Kissimmee. And the important thing is that Disney World is located just a few miles from the crossing point of Interstate 4 and Sunshine State Parkway, Florida's major highways carrying motorists east and west and north and south through the center of the state.

The sketches and plans you will see today are simply a starting point: our first overall thinking about Disney World. Everything in this room may change time and time again as we move ahead, but the basic philosophy of what we're planning for Disney World is going to remain very much as it is right now.

We know what our goals are. We know what we hope to accomplish. And believe me, it's the most exciting and challenging assignment we've ever tackled at Walt Disney Productions.

Today I want to share with you some of our ideas for Disney World. Now the prologue for this film told you some of the philosophy that made Disneyland in California what it is today. Of course, there will be another amusement theme park in Florida similar to the one in California. We're now developing a master plan that encompasses the theme park and all the facilities around it that will serve the tourist: hotels, motels, and a variety of recreational activity. In fact, just this little area alone is five times the size of Disneyland in California.

As you can see on this master plan, the theme park and all the other tourist facilities fill just one small area of our enormous Florida project. According to this scale, I am six miles tall! Now, it's twelve miles from here up to here and the whole area encompasses 27,400 acres. That is forty-three square miles: twice the size of the island of Manhattan. Now, the area we propose to develop is between the Reedy Creek swamp and the Bonnet Creek swamp. So one thing we don't need is a fence to protect us from trespassers.

Here in Florida we have something special we never enjoyed at Disneyland: the blessing of size. There's enough land here to hold all the ideas and plans we could possibly imagine.

Right now our plans include an airport of the future (down here in Osceola County), an entrance complex where all visitors will enter Disney World, an industrial park area covering about 1000 acres, and of course, the theme park area way up here. And all these varied activities around the Disney World will be tied together with a high-speed rapid transit system running almost the full length of the property.

But the most exciting, by far the most important part of our Florida project—in fact, the heart of everything we'll be doing in Disney World—will be our experimental prototype city of tomorrow. We call it E.P.C.O.T. spelled E-P-C-O-T: Experimental Prototype Community of Tomorrow. Here it is in larger scale.

E.P.C.O.T. will take its cue from the new ideas and new technologies that are now emerging from the creative centers of American industry. It will be a community of tomorrow that will never be completed, but will always be introducing, and testing, and demonstrating new materials and new systems. And E.P.C.O.T. will always be a showcase to the world of the ingenuity and imagination of American free enterprise.

I don't believe there is a challenge anywhere in the world that's more important to people everywhere than finding solutions to the problems of our cities.

But where do we begin? How do we start answering this great challenge? Well, we're convinced we must start with the public need. And the need is not just for curing the old ills of old cities. We think the need is for starting from scratch on virgin land and building a special kind of new community. So that's what E.P.C.O.T. is: an Experimental Prototype Community that will always be in the state of becoming. It will never cease to be a living blueprint of the future where people actually live a life they can't find anyplace else in the world.

Everything in E.P.C.O.T. will be dedicated to the happiness of the people who live, work, and play here, and those who come here from around the world to visit our living showcase.

We don't presume to know all the answers. In fact, we're counting on the cooperation of American industry to provide their very best thinking during the planning and the creation of our Experimental Prototype Community of Tomorrow. And most important of all, when E.P.C.O.T. has become a reality and we find the need for technologies that don't even exist today, it's our hope that E.P.C.O.T. will stimulate American industry to develop new solutions that will meet the needs of people expressed right here in this experimental community.

Well, that's our basic philosophy for E.P.C.O.T. By now, I'm sure you're wondering how people will live and work and move around in our community of tomorrow, so in the next few minutes we will go into detail about some of our preliminary sketches and layouts. Remember though, as I said earlier, this is just the beginning! With that thought in mind, let's have a look.[21]

Most of Walt's on-screen pitch was complete. The rest of the twenty-four-minute film was dedicated to the details dreamed up for E.P.C.O.T., complete with concept art and animation. Let's dive in:

No city of today will serve as the guide for the city of tomorrow. E.P.C.O.T. will be a planned environment demonstrating to the world what American communities can accomplish through proper control of planning and design.

E.P.C.O.T. begins with an idea new among cities built since the birth of the automobile. We call it the radial plan. Picture a wheel: like the spokes of a wheel, the city fans out along a series of radials from a bustling hub at the center of E.P.C.O.T.

A network of transportation systems radiate from the central hub carrying people to and from the heart of the city. These transportation systems circulate to and through four primary spheres of activity surrounding the central core. First, the area of business and commerce . . . next, the high-density apartment housing . . . then the broad greenbelt and recreation lands . . . and finally the low-density, neighborhood residential streets.

E.P.C.O.T.'s dynamic urban center will offer the excitement and variety of activities found only in the metropolitan cities: cultural, social, business, and entertainment.

Among its major features will be a cosmopolitan hotel and convention center towering thirty or more stories. Shopping areas where stores and whole streets recreate the character and adventure of places 'round the world . . . theaters for dramatic and musical productions . . . restaurants and a variety of nightlife attractions. And a wide range of office buildings, some containing services required by E.P.C.O.T.'s residents, but most of them designed especially to suit local and regional needs of major corporations.

But most important, this entire fifty acres of city streets and buildings will be completely enclosed. In this climate-controlled environment, shoppers, theatergoers, and people just out for a stroll will enjoy ideal weather conditions, protected day and night from rain, heat and cold, and humidity.

Here the pedestrian will be king, free to walk and browse without fear of motorized vehicles. Only electric powered vehicles will travel above the streets of E.P.C.O.T.'s central city.

This towering motel is the visual center of E.P.C.O.T., a shining jewel at the center of the city. It will offer tourists and vacationers not only the most modern guest rooms and convention facilities, but also a seven-acre recreation deck located high above the pedestrian and shopping areas of the city.

But hidden from view, directly beneath the hotel, is another kind of vital center: E.P.C.O.T.'s transportation lobby. Although out of sight to hotel guests, this transportation terminal will play a key role in the City of Tomorrow's ability to meet the needs of both visitor and resident.

E.P.C.O.T. CONCEPT MAP

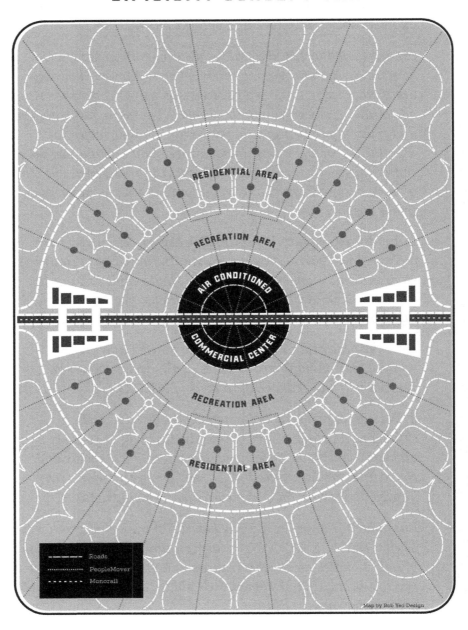

RESIDENTIAL AREA

RECREATION AREA

AIR CONDITIONED

COMMERCIAL CENTER

RECREATION AREA

RESIDENTIAL AREA

Roads
PeopleMover
Monorail

Map by Rob Yeo Design

Two separate but interconnecting transit systems will move people into and out of E.P.C.O.T. in speed, safety, and comfort through the central terminal. Both are electrically powered: the high-speed monorail for rapid transit over longer distances, and a concept new to the American City for shorter travel distances, the WEDway PeopleMover.

Automobiles and trucks will not be barred from E.P.C.O.T. In fact, a vast armada of vehicles will continuously flow through the heart of the community, traveling below the pedestrian level on roadways reserved for specific types of vehicles.

Let's look at another view of E.P.C.O.T.'s transportation hub and see how traffic flows through the heart of the city on three separate levels.

At the bottom of the stack is the truck route, reserved for supply vehicles. Trucks will have easy access to all loading docks and service elevators for the delivery of commercial goods.

The middle level is the automobile thruway, exclusively for cars. Adjacent to the roadway are parking areas for the convenience of hotel guests. For the motorist just driving through, no stoplight will ever slow the constant flow of traffic through the center of E.P.C.O.T.

But automobiles and freeways will not be E.P.C.O.T.'s major way of entering and leaving the city. The transportation heartbeat of EPCOT will be the two electric powered systems— monorail and WEDway—that radiate to and from the transportation lobby, and the key system in this coordinated network will be the WEDway PeopleMover.

The first PeopleMover installation is already in daily operation at Disneyland. On peak days, it carries nearly 40,000 passengers. The cars you see here are approximately 5/8ths scale, considerably smaller than full-sized passenger cars would be for city use.

E.P.C.O.T.'s PeopleMover is a silent, all-electric system that never stops running. These cars continue to move even while passengers are disembarking or stepping aboard. Power is supplied through a series of motors embedded in the track, completely independent of the cars. No single car can ever break down and cause a rush hour traffic jam in E.P.C.O.T. Because the cars run continuously, there will be no waiting in stations for the WEDway PeopleMover; the next car is always ready.

Now let's go back to the Transportation Lobby and see how the WEDway will travel along one radial between the center of E.P.C.O.T. and a typical residential area.

Leaving the Transportation Lobby, the WEDway trains travel above the downtown streets. Within minutes, the WEDway passes through the first station. Many people who work in the offices and stores of E.P.C.O.T.'s city center board the WEDway here for their trip home. Some people leave the WEDway here, too: they live in E.P.C.O.T.'s high-density apartments surrounding the metropolitan center.

Most passengers who ride the WEDway live beyond the apartments and stay aboard the PeopleMover as it crosses E.P.C.O.T.'s sheltering greenbelt.

E.P.C.O.T.'s greenbelt is more than just a broad expanse of beautiful lawns and walks and trees. Here too are the communities' varied recreation facilities, its playgrounds for children, its churches, and its schools.

Beyond the greenbelt are E.P.C.O.T's neighborhood areas of single-family homes. This is one radial neighborhood. Here and throughout the community, residents returning from work or shopping will disembark from the WEDway at stations located conveniently just a few steps from where they live.

The homes are located in a wide green area that provides light recreation activities for adults and play areas for children. Circulating through this area are footpaths reserved for pedestrians, electric carts, and bicycles. Children going to and from schools and playgrounds will use these paths, always completely safe and separated from the automobile.

The resident leaving home in his automobile will drive down a street reserved for motor vehicles. He then enters a one-way road that circles the city center. This road carries the motorist onto the main throughway connecting E.P.C.O.T. with other points in Disney World and with Florida's nearby network of major highways. But most E.P.C.O.T. residents will drive their automobiles only on weekend pleasure trips. From all over the community residents going to their jobs converge by WEDway on the Center City. Many work downtown in offices, stores, and shops, but most employees go beyond the city core to their jobs. From the Transportation Lobby, monorail trains carry employees either to the theme park or to E.P.C.O.T.'s one thousand-acre industrial park.

At this central station in the industrial complex, passengers disembark from the monorail and again board WEDway cars that radiate to each facility. This industrial complex will provide employment for many people who live in E.P.C.O.T. But it will mean much more, not only for this community but also for American industry. Here the Disney staff will work with individual companies to create a showcase of industry at work.

In attractive park-like settings, the six million people who visit Disney World each year will look behind the scenes at *experimental prototype plants, research and development laboratories, and computer centers for major corporations.*

So this is E.P.C.O.T. the heart of Disney World. In other parts of the country, a community the size of this prototype could become part of an entire city complex composed of many such communities, planned and built a few miles apart. In Disney World, about 20,000 people will actually live in E.P.C.O.T. Their homes will be built in ways that permit ease of change so that new products may continuously be demonstrated. Their schools will welcome new ideas so that everyone who grows up in E.P.C.O.T. will have skills in pace with today's world.

E.P.C.O.T. will be a working community with employment for all. And everyone who lives here will have a responsibility to help keep this community an exciting living blueprint of the future.[22]

Walt came back on screen for a wrap up:

That's the starting point for our Experimental Prototype Community of Tomorrow. And now, where do we go from these preliminary plans and sketches?

Well, a project like this is so vast in scope that no one company alone could make it a reality. But if we can bring together the technical know-how of American industry and the creative imagination of the Disney organization, I'm confident we can create—right here in Disney World—a showcase to the world of the American free enterprise system.

I believe we can build a community that more people will talk about and come to look at than any other area in the world. And with your cooperation, I'm sure that the Experimental Prototype Community of Tomorrow can influence the future of city living for generations to come. It's an exciting challenge; a once-in-a-lifetime opportunity for everyone who participates. Speaking for myself and the entire Disney organization, we're ready to go right now![23]

You can now see why Walt wanted full legal control over his land. The creation of a theme park was tangential, merely an attraction to lure people to his new city.

If anyone else had proposed this idea, he or she would have probably been rebuffed. But the fact that this was *the* Walt Disney, maybe, just maybe, he could pull this off, and we would be living in a city of tomorrow within the next decade.

As fate would have it, on November 2, 1966, just a few days after filming his presentation, Walt was admitted to Saint Joseph's Hospital. The studio released the following statement:

Walt Disney was initially admitted to the hospital on Nov. 2 for treatment and preliminary examination of an old polo injury. During the preliminary examination, a lesion was discovered on his left lung.

Surgery was decided upon and performed the next week. A tumor was found to have caused an abscess which, in the opinion of the doctors required a pneumonectomy.

Within four to six weeks, Mr. Disney should be back on a full schedule. There is no reason to predict any recurrence of the problem or curtailment of his future activities.[24]

Just over a month after that press release, Walt Disney passed away on December 15, 1966. The E.P.C.O.T. film had been his swan song and the second-to-last time he was on camera.

Walt never was able to resume his full-time duties at the studio, as the press release suggested he would be able to. Tragically, all his years of smoking cigarettes had caught up with him.

At the age of sixty-five, Walter Elias Disney passed away at Saint Joseph's Hospital located across the street from his studio, at 9:35 a.m.; his death was attributed to acute circulatory collapse.[25]

Walt Disney was a once-in-a-lifetime personality. He changed things in our society on par with Henry Ford, an icon of his day, and Steve Jobs, an icon of our day. Walt made it into *Time* magazine's "*Time* 100: The Most Important People of the Century."

With Walt gone, the project was now in jeopardy. The state of Florida was left wondering not only what could have been, but what, if anything, would be?

A week after Walt's death, Helliwell met with some members of the Orange County Legislative Delegation. He informed them that Disney intended to seek a charter from the state for two municipalities. The entire project would still move forward.[26]

Roy stepped up to lead the venture. Around the time of the initial land purchases, Roy was seriously contemplating retirement. This was not an option now. He had a new task, one that meant more to him than just about anything else in his life—make sure his brother's final dream came true.

Roy wasn't sure if he could fully accomplish Walt's E.P.C.O.T. dream. But he would certainly try. He gathered the group of Disney executives and told them, "We're going to finish this project, and we're going to do it just the way Walt wanted it. Don't you ever forget it. I want every one of you to do just exactly what you were going to do when Walt was alive."[27]

Roy even decided on a name change for the project. It wouldn't be called Disneyland Two or Disneyland East; it wouldn't even be called Disney World.

Roy said it was going to be called Walt Disney World, so everyone would be reminded of the creative genius who dreamed up this enterprise.

Losing Walt wasn't the only major change at the top of the project. Things were different on the Florida side too—Governor Burns was no longer at the helm of the state.

As it turned out, aligning himself with Disney didn't do much for his political career. In the 1966 Democratic primary, the mayor of

Miami, Bob High, defeated Burns. In the general election, High lost to Republican Claude Kirk Jr.

This outcome was a shock to those working on the project. Burns had consulted often with Disney and made several trips out to California. He had provided his full support and complete access to his staff and personnel.[28]

Burns left office during the first week of January 1967, leaving lingering questions about how receptive the new governor would be to Disney having its own slice of supremacy in central Florida.

Claude Kirk Jr. ran for office on a campaign pledge to be "tough on crime in the streets."[29] Once he took office, he thought it would be a good idea to travel to California to see how the city of Anaheim handled the influx of "scoundrels" coming into the area because of Disneyland.[30]

This didn't appear to be a good start for Disney's relationship with the new head of the state. While in California, Kirk requested to meet with Governor Ronald Reagan.

Reagan was a longtime friend of Walt Disney's. He was also a member of Disneyland's opening day festivities, as a television host.

As a longtime Disney ally, Reagan would have nothing but positive things to say about Disneyland's impact on the community and the state.

Donn Tatum and Card Walker—who continued to be members of Disney's new leadership group post-Walt—spent the day with Governors Reagan and Kirk. They discussed Disneyland, Anaheim, and naturally, central Florida, and how the area would be impacted by Walt Disney World.[31]

The day went smoothly and had Disney feeling better about its new partner. The company was finally set to move forward with its plans—of which the public hadn't heard about since Walt's press conference back in '65.

On February 2, 1967, all of that changed when Disney held a press conference in Winter Park, Florida at the town's Park West Theatre.

The public was presented with Walt's E.P.C.O.T. film. To close out the evening, Governor Kirk, Roy, and Roy's trusted group of executives expounded on Walt's dream.[32]

Nearly 1,000 people were packed into the theater, including Kirk's newly assembled cabinet, the state and local legislature, members of the local and national press, and anyone else important enough to get a ticket to attend.

Governor Kirk spoke briefly, as did Disney's top brass, and then the film started. In the film, Walt captivated the audience, despite being in the throes of lung cancer.

Like children watching a new Mickey Mouse cartoon, you could hear and feel the excitement from the audience, many of which held the power to embrace and accept this project or veto and derail it.

Park West Theatre, Winter Park, Florida.
February 1967. The Florida Memory Project.

As the theater lights came on, Roy stepped into the spotlight, and out from his brother's looming shadow. He was now the pitchman and the money man. Roy got right down to business:

> *Wasn't that a dream? Doesn't that stagger you? . . . Our corporation is dedicated to making Walt Disney's dream a reality. But it cannot be done without the help of you people here in Florida . . . We must have a solid legal foundation before we can proceed with Disney World . . . This foundation can be assured by the legislative proposals we are presenting to the next session of the Florida legislature. If these requests are granted, I believe that we can make the new theme park a reality by 1971.*[33]

Roy spoke briefly about the details. The project would be done in phases. Disney was prepared to invest over $600 million into it. Phase one would be the theme park, at a cost of $100 million. Phase two would be E.P.C.O.T. and all of the other ideas.[34]

Next, Donn Tatum spoke. He said that, a few days prior to the press conference, Disney had presented the Orange and Osceola County governments with three acts to review. The first two acts were the same—the creation of two municipalities, the cities of Lake Buena Vista and Bay Lake.

The third act would be for the creation of the Reedy Creek Improvement District, which would encompass the entire Disney property.

In its simplest form, these acts basically gave Disney complete legal power and control over its land—drainage, utilities, sewer systems, construction, public transportation, airports, fire and EMS, and so forth.

In addition to control, the act had a provision allowing Disney to issue bonds to fund necessary improvements throughout its district.[35]

With the exception of the widening of Interstate 4 and State Road 530 adjacent to the land and the completion of a new interchange from State Road 530 onto the property (Disney's research stated that

95 percent of the cars would enter the Disney property from Interstate 4 and Road 530), this project would not require a nickel of tax money or any tax concessions.[36]

As Helliwell was quoted, "There are no gimmicks, no tax concessions, no demands for concessions and no curves."[37]

So, what would the state of Florida get out of the deal? Governor Kirk said Disney's projections revealed the following:

During its first ten years of operation, Walt Disney World will directly generate $6.6 billion in measurable economic benefits for the state of Florida as a whole.

This impact would be felt in all parts of the state, primarily in terms of increased tourist volume, and the facilities and service employment this will require.

The impact of new construction, employment, industrial employment and the additional retail and service employment created throughout the state, from these payrolls, 80 percent, or approximately $1.8 billion, will be spent in the central Florida area for retail goods and services, and other living expenses.[38]

At the conclusion of the event, the Governor and Roy took their show on the road. The two flew up to Jacksonville and taped a presentation that was packaged with Walt's E.P.C.O.T. film for television viewers.

This program aired throughout the entire state of Florida, informing residents of Disney's plan and helping to garner excitement for the project.

Disney's legislation was officially introduced in both the Florida House and Senate on April 17, 1967.

On the morning the package was presented to lawmakers, Helliwell spoke briefly to them about the project, and he even arranged for the E.P.C.O.T. film to play on the House and the Senate floor.

In the weeks after that presentation, government officials had the opportunity to look over Disney's 481 pages of legislation.

Aside from a few changes requested by the telephone and electric company, and a few other details, the bill overwhelmingly passed both arms of the government on May 5, 1967, and was sent to the governor for his signature.[39]

The E.P.C.O.T. film had done its job. On May 12, 1967, Claude R. Kirk Jr.—the thirty-sixth governor of Florida—gave Disney the keys to its kingdom by signing into legislation Disney's two towns and the overall improvement district.

At the signing ceremony, in the Governor's mansion, Roy, the Governor, Donn Tatum, and Robert Foster walked together on their way to sign the documents. The Governor stopped for a brief moment turned to Roy with a straight face and said, "Roy, I have studied your legislation, there is one serious omission." According to Foster, "Roy, somewhat astonished inquired what it might be. The governor replied, 'there was no provision in the kingdom for the crown.'"[40]

Roy Disney and group watching as Governor Claude Kirk signs the Disney bill at the Governor's mansion - Tallahassee, Florida. May 12, 1967. The Florida Memory Project.

As the Governor joked, Disney got everything it wanted. Its quasi-government package was passed without even a debate.

In defense of what Disney received, Helliwell often remarked it wasn't unusual for the state to create these districts.

He was partially correct. In terms of the drainage district, the state did regularly authorize those. However, this was the first time the state had combined three districts into one very powerful super district for a private-sector business to operate.

At the time, and totally off the record, some in the government were a little concerned about what passing this legislation could mean in a worst-case scenario for the state.

An attorney for Orange County, who negotiated with Disney said:

The county was kind of shaken by the degree of control they desired . . . the fear was that Disney was so large, and had so much land, that the county might have a competing government exercising government powers that would impair the county's ability to control its affairs . . . it was a problem philosophically, because we were giving government powers to a business. No one wanted to negotiate to the point that we stopped them from coming.[41]

Years later a chorus of doubts would come to surface. Many comments were in the realm of "to be against it was to vote against motherhood and apple pie."[42]

Henry Land, who was the chair of the House Appropriations Committee at the time, said, "If I didn't support it, I would have been lynched." He didn't see much danger in what Disney was trying to accomplish. But years later he said it was the worst thing to happen to the state of Florida, as it ended up giving Disney too many powers. He admitted later to not reading a word of the legislation when it was proposed.[43]

The best of these stories involved the president of the Senate, Verle Pope. Disney hired a former state representative, J. J. Griffin, to lobby on its behalf.[44]

L-R: Don Tatum, Roy Disney, Jack Sayers,
William Potter on Disney property, 1967.

Griffin scheduled a meeting with the powerful Pope to explain to him what Disney was hoping to accomplish and to breakdown its proposed legislation.

As the meeting commenced and Griffin started to explain Disney's position, Pope interrupted him and said he had one question: "Is it good for Florida?" Griffin said yes, he believed it would be.[45]

Pope said, "Well, that's good enough for me," and that was the end of the meeting.[46]

If there was a bit of "buyer's remorse" or some Monday morning quarterbacking, that's probably to be expected, and it really didn't matter, as it was a done deal.

From the Disney side of things, it was very pleased with the outcome. It had been a long three years from the time the land was purchased to when the legislation was signed.

Initial projections for opening day were sometime in 1971. With all the t's crossed and i's dotted, it was time for Disney to start building its kingdom.

Chapter **8**

FABRICATING THE FIEFDOM

May 30, 1967, was the official groundbreaking day for Walt Disney World. As mentioned in chapter six, some experimental land clearing, drainage, and reclamation work started back in October of 1965.[1]

Disney consistently worked on the project in some capacity during the year and a half leading up to the passage of the Reedy Creek legislation.

In February of 1966, Disney opened its first office in downtown Orlando, operating under the name Compass East Corporation.[2]

This office was staffed by a young attorney by the name of Phil Smith. Smith's new office handled any ancillary legal or construction issues, such as filing permits and things of that nature.

Mr. Smith has a few Disney distinctions to his name. He was the first official cast member hired for Walt Disney World. He also helped hire the first female cast member, Julia Switlick. (Julia was hired as a legal secretary in the summer of 1965 but didn't start work until January 1, 1966.)

When asked about her time at Disney, Switlick commented that her job interview was pretty unusual. She didn't really know who her employer would be or what they were doing, yet she took the job anyway.

She said she met with a law firm to discuss a position, but the details were very vague and hush hush. "I was worried I might be working for the communists. In those days, just saying someone was communist was the worst thing you could do."[3]

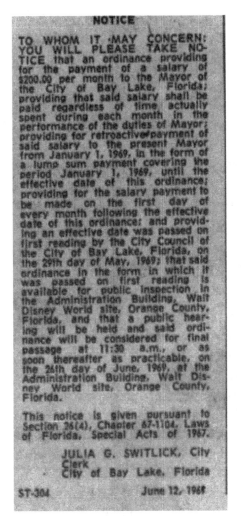

NOTICE

TO WHOM IT MAY CONCERN: YOU WILL PLEASE TAKE NOTICE that an ordinance providing for the payment of a salary of $200.00 per month to the Mayor of the City of Bay Lake, Florida; providing that said salary shall be paid regardless of time actually spent during each month in the performance of the duties of Mayor; providing for retroactive payment of said salary to the present Mayor from January 1, 1969, in the form of a lump sum payment covering the period January 1, 1969, until the effective date of this ordinance; providing for the salary payment to be made on the first day of every month following the effective date of this ordinance; and providing an effective date was passed on first reading by the City Council of the City of Bay Lake, Florida, on the 29th day of May, 1969; that said ordinance in the form in which it was passed on first reading is available for public inspection in the Administration Building, Walt Disney World site, Orange County, Florida, and that a public hearing will be held and said ordinance will be considered for final passage at 11:30 a.m., or as soon thereafter as practicable, on the 26th day of June, 1969, at the Administration Building, Walt Disney World site, Orange County, Florida.

This notice is given pursuant to Section 26(4), Chapter 67-1104, Laws of Florida, Special Acts of 1967.

JULIA G. SWITLICK, City Clerk
City of Bay Lake, Florida

ST-304   June 12, 1969

Phil Smith was also the first person to live on the Disney property. From June 1966 to November 1968, Smith and his family lived in the house on what was formerly the Bronson property—this was where Walt had his picnic the day after the November 1965 press conference.[4]

Smith wasn't the last Disney employee to live at Walt Disney World. Today there is still a small group of employees and retired employees who live in the city of Bay Lake (population of 47, according to the 2010 census) and the city of Lake Buena Vista (population of 10, according to the 2010 census).

Each city has a Mayor and a town council composed of the residents who live there. Back in 1969, a legal notice (written by Julia Switlick) was published announcing an ordinance for the Mayor of Bay Lake to receive a salary of $200 a month.[5]

The residents of Bay Lake, home to four Disney theme parks, live on a gated street just a stone's throw from Bay Lake, about a mile northeast of Magic Kingdom.

Those who reside in the city of Lake Buena Vista live not too far from Disney Springs.

It's not entirely clear how one gets to be selected as a resident of these company towns. Those residing there own their homes but rent their land from Disney for seventy-five dollars a month.[6]

There is no formal lease, and history shows they can live on site for an indeterminate amount of time.[7]

Obviously, the residents are vetted and carefully chosen, as they vote on referendums put forth by the Reedy Creek Improvement District (RCID).

As we know, the RCID governs the two cities and the entire Disney property. The district covers just about every function any other city government in Florida covers.

The RCID issues building permits, operates utility systems, handles drainage, maintains the property, and even operates the fire and EMS services. Police powers were not included in the legislation passed in 1967; therefore, the Orange County Sheriff Office is the primary responder for law enforcement matters within the district.[8]

RCID employs approximately 300 full-time staff members and funds its operations from taxes and fees imposed within its boundaries, which support the infrastructure. The district collected over $54 million in ad valorem taxes in 2004, with the majority (86 percent) paid by the Walt Disney Company and its affiliates.[9]

During this same period, the district collected $147.7 million in fees for providing public utility services, such as electricity, gas, water, and wastewater.[10]

According to Section 4 of the Reedy Creek Improvement District's charter, a board of supervisors shall be the governing body of the district.

This board consists of five members, who serve a term of four years. All of the members of the board must be owners of land within the district.[11]

In order to fulfill this requirement of the RCID charter, members of the board of supervisors are deeded an undeveloped parcel of land within the district for their term on the board. When their term is over, this land goes back to the RCID.

As far as who owns what within the RCID boundary, here's a breakdown from the mid-2000s. RCID owns approximately 28.8 percent of the land in the district (7,191 acres); the Walt Disney Company owns 68.8 percent (17,119 acres); the state of Florida owns 2.2 percent (550.3 acres); and other entities such as Orange County, Palm Hospitality Co., and the Celebration company own the remaining 0.44 percent (109.5 acres).[12]

This key piece of land ownership and voting control (each one acre owned equals one vote) goes back to Paul Helliwell. When the legislation was being drafted, Helliwell insisted that the super district have voting rights assigned by acreage owned within their district.[13]

This setup allows Disney to stay in control of the area forever, or at least until it ceases being the majority owner.[14]

Ironically, back in those early construction and development years, there was a pretty important Disney employee who wasn't living on site, nor was he a member of the RCID board of supervisors: Roy O. Disney.

In 1968 Roy had five lakeside cottage homes built on Tibet Bay Drive, which is about ten miles from Disney property—in 2001 Disney sold the homes to Arnold Palmer Bay Hill Country Club and Lodge.[15]

LAND OWNERSHIP WITHIN RCID

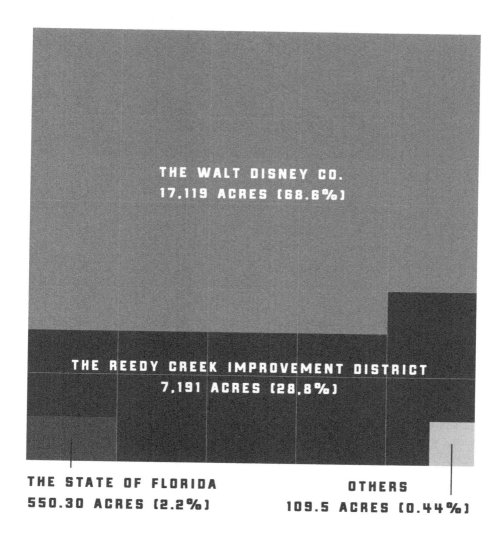

THE WALT DISNEY CO.
17,119 ACRES (68.6%)

THE REEDY CREEK IMPROVEMENT DISTRICT
7,191 ACRES (28.8%)

THE STATE OF FLORIDA
550.30 ACRES (2.2%)

OTHERS
109.5 ACRES (0.44%)

As of mid-2000s

The off-site Disney cottages.

Roy and a handful of Disney executives—most notably Donn Tatum, Card Walker, and Admiral Joe Fowler—lived there.

Roy and Admiral Joe lived next door to each other, further solidifying their close relationship. Over the next three years, these two men, along with another guy named Joe (General Joe Potter), worked diligently to bring Walt Disney World to life.

Both Joes were military men. After they served Uncle Sam in the United States government, the men went on to serve Uncle Walt and his government in Florida.

General Joe Potter (birth name William Potter, nickname Joe) was an integral part of the early team working on the Florida land acquisition and helped with the legislation to form the RCID.

In fact, after it was formed, Potter was elected president of the board of supervisors and district administer of the RCID in October of 1968.

The General joined Disney after working as the executive vice president of the 1964–1965 New York World's Fair.

Prior to the fair, President Dwight D. Eisenhower appointed Joe as the governor of the Panama Canal Zone, and president of the Panama Canal Corporation, for four years.[16]

A graduate of the Massachusetts Institute of Technology with a degree in civil engineering, General Joe was a logistics planner for the invasion of Normandy and commanded the troop section of the Propaganda and Psychological Warfare Division during World War II.[17]

After the war Potter supervised many of the Army's engineering projects, from military construction in Alaska to the Missouri River Project where, as head engineer, he directed flood control, navigation, and water use for an area covering one-sixth of the country.[18]

Clearly, the General was great at strategy, planning, and water control, which is why Walt wanted him to take the lead down in Florida. Walt gave Joe the title of Vice President of Florida Planning.[19]

Potter worked behind the scenes, overseeing the construction of the park's infrastructure, which included underground utilities, a sewer system, and a power grid, along with water treatment plants and land reclamation measures.

The other Joe, Rear Admiral Joseph W. Fowler, was at the helm of just about everything else Potter wasn't handling, including the creation of the theme park itself, the hotels, transportation, and the like.

Admiral Fowler had graduated second in his class from the US Naval Academy in 1917. Like General Potter, Fowler was also a graduate of MIT, with a master's degree in naval architecture.

Admiral Fowler fought in both World War I and World War II. He spent an extensive amount of time in China where he roomed with Edward, Prince of Wales, on a British gunship steaming up the Yangtze River.[20]

When he wasn't in battle, Joe designed and supervised the construction of twenty-nine warships, from submarines to aircraft carriers—most notably the USS Lexington and the USS Saratoga.[21]

After 35 years in the US Navy—and far too many accolades and accomplishments to list—Rear Admiral Joseph W. Fowler retired from service in 1948.

With his military career behind him, what should such a distinguished and motivated man do now that he was retired? How about help build a revolutionary theme park in Southern California known as Disneyland?

After doing some consulting work for the government for a few years post-retirement, a new opportunity popped up, and well, he sort of just went with the flow of things. Let's read about it from the Admiral himself:

One of the contractors I had happened to work for was located in San Francisco, California at Stanford Research Institute and the head of research was a fellow named C. V. Wood. We became very good friends socially, as well as professionally. So, when I came back to California, in '52 I guess it was, I established my own work at that time in San Francisco, living in a ranch house.

I called up Woody, wanted to say hello. So, he said: "I'm bringing a friend with me." Didn't say who it was. It was Walt Disney. Walt had the habit when he [was thinking about hiring] somebody, that he was going [to the meeting] incognito and talking with them [as a friend], so I knew nothing [about Walt's plans to hire me].

They came up to the ranch and we talked for an hour. Walt was always interested in toy railroads, so that you could scale it and ride it. There's one in an orchard in Los Gatos. We went down and rode that. And we came back, now at this time I had known Walt for two hours and he said: "Hey your name is Joe?" and I said: "Yes." And he said: "My name is Walt. No more of this Admiral and this business. Joe and Walt."

And so it was. Now he said: "I'm going to send you a ticket the first of the week. I want you to come down and see the studio and maybe get the feel of things and help us build Disneyland."

I told my wife: "I don't know anything about Hollywood, but I've got an invitation to see the studios, down to see it. I've got a ticket and everything. I'll be down and I'll be back tomorrow night."

I went down, came to Burbank and they took me up to Walt's office. We talked for about fifteen minutes, and he was called out to see the morning rushes . . . now he said: "Make yourself at home, but I'll be back shortly. And if you want anything, press the button, someone will get it for you. Coffee, orange juice, Wall Street Journal, *and so forth."*

He'd been gone for about ten or fifteen minutes, and a lady stuck her head in the door and said: "Your name's Joe Fowler?" "Yes" "Come with me" "Sure," I said. We walked down the corridor, and she said: "Here's your office. And here's an office on the other side of the corridor for the contractors who want to talk to you about building Disneyland."

I was in the business for three weeks before he mentioned salary or anything. That's how I came to work for Walt Disney for twenty-five years.

I didn't care about the salary. I had my retired pay, and I loved the studio. Roy used to say I was the longest temporary employee they ever had.[22]

How's that for an interview, onboarding and first day of work all wrapped into one?! From that day on, Joe oversaw construction of Disneyland, and he went on to manage its operations after it opened.

Years later Walt joked that "little by little we got Fowler trapped into this thing [Disneyland]!"[23]

Just weeks before Disneyland was set to open, Walt was out of money. The banks wouldn't loan him another dollar, all of his insurance policies were cashed in, and the park still wasn't complete.

In the final days leading up to the scheduled opening of Disneyland, Walt secured a much-needed loan to keep things on track:

"Joe Fowler loaned Walt Disney some of his own personal money to keep Disneyland afloat," recalls Fowler's longtime assistant Patricia Branham. "He did that on a personal level for [Walt]." Fowler himself never spoke publicly about this loan, most likely out of a sense of propriety. Neither did Walt Disney.[24]

Walt and Joe had a special relationship. The Admiral often reminisced about some of his capers with Walt in Florida:

Walt didn't live long enough to see us break ground in Disney World, but he used to travel all over the property with me in a Jeep. He loved it. I remember he wanted to see how Disney World would look from the top of the Contemporary Hotel. So we got the biggest damned utility crane in Florida, and the two of us got into the bucket and they hoisted us straight up to where the lounge at the top of the Contemporary would be.

I was so damn busy hanging on, hoping to get down, and he was so enthusiastic: 'Oh Joe, look at this! This is going to be great!' He could visualize it all. I could see enough to realize that everything [in the plans] was properly located. Oh my, he was a wonderful man.[25]

There are a few more Disney executives we need to get acquainted, or better acquainted, with before this story soldiers on. You may remember Card Walker and Donn Tatum from earlier in the book, but Dick Nunis was another important Disney executive.

During the early stages of planning and before Walt passed away, he had already tapped Tatum and Walker to have substantial roles in the Florida project.

Tatum was a Stanford and Oxford educated attorney. He joined Disney in the mid-1950s, and as mentioned, he eventually rose to become a vice president and member of the board of directors while both Disney brothers were still alive.

Tatum was also the first president of Walt Disney World, and after Roy's death, Donn succeeded him as Chairman and CEO of the Walt Disney Company.[26]

Esmond Cardon "Card" Walker was educated at UCLA and started his tenure at Disney as a worker in the mailroom. Card worked his way up from the bottom, and in 1956 Walt named him Vice President of Advertising and Sales.

By 1965 Card was appointed Vice President of Marketing, followed by Executive Vice President of Operations in 1967 and Executive Vice President and Chief Operating Officer in 1968.

His next stop would be as the president of the company, a position he held for five years. His last stop would be as the chairman of the board in 1980.[27]

Richard A. Nunis attended the University of Southern California on a football scholarship. At the time, one of his teammates was Ron Miller, who was married to Walt's daughter, Diane.

After hearing Miller talk about Disneyland a few times, Nunis applied for a summer job there. Hired before the park opened, Dick worked to train employees. During the late 1950s through the early 1960s, he worked in a variety of capacities throughout the park.

In 1961 he became the director of operations at Disneyland and by 1968 he was the vice president of operations. Nunis was eventually named Executive Vice President of Walt Disney World and Disneyland.

He ultimately retired as the president and chairman of Walt Disney Attractions—forty-four years to the day that he was hired at Disneyland.[28]

During an interview in 1988, Nunis commented that "without Joe Potter there would be no Walt Disney World today. Joe was a man Walt Disney was very fond of."[29]

Let's read about how Joe and the boys built Walt's Magic Kingdom.

Very early estimates put the cost of building Walt Disney World at around $100 million; this number was floated out to the media several times.

One source of funding came in the form of corporate sponsors. Disney perfected the art of sponsorship at Disneyland and at the New York World's Fair.

It was pretty simple and straightforward—companies paid a fee and then had representation in the park.

Disney initially pegged its sponsorship money at about $30 million, leaving the company to come up with $70 million to complete the project. These were the estimates from 1965–1966.[30]

By 1969–1970, when Disney was ready to go full steam ahead with construction, final cost estimates swelled nearly fourfold. With the buzz surrounding the project, Disney had little trouble finding corporate sponsors looking to get in on the ground floor.

Corporations would pay, at a minimum, $40,000 a year to be represented and aligned with the Disney brand on site.

That fee didn't include whatever construction costs would be incurred, which were usually in the neighborhood of another $35,000. At this $40,000 mark, the sponsors would get leased space in a shared building.[31]

For about $100,000 a year, along with the absorption of the entire cost of construction (roughly $250,000), they could be featured in their own building where they were free to promote and sell their products alongside Disney's.[32]

One of the early sponsors was GAF, a film manufacturer. As the official film of Walt Disney World, GAF committed to spending more than a million dollars over the first five years of the park's operation.

Gulf Oil signed a ten-year deal to provide fuel and service centers within Disney property. Borden Inc. was under contract to handle Disney's milk and ice cream needs. Smucker's, Coca-Cola, RCA, Eastern Airlines, and over a dozen other notable corporations rounded out the early list of corporate partners.[33]

Sponsorship dollars were now just a small portion of the money Disney needed as the park's price tag swelled. The bulk of the funding came from Roy's financial ingenuity.

On January 17, 1968, Disney issued $40 million in convertible subordinated debentures, due January 15, 1993. Roy did this again in 1969 for an additional $50 million, due March 1, 1994.[34]

The debentures were converted into Disney stock once the stock hit $65 a share and then they were immediately retired.[35]

In anticipation of the opening of Walt Disney World, Disney's shares moved pretty aggressively. The debentures issued in 1968 and 1969 were retired by 1970 when Disney's stock price moved above the conversion price.[36]

In May of 1968, Disney entered into a revolving credit line with Bank of America—Disney had been banking with it since the 1930s when Walt took out loans to fund *Snow White and the Seven Dwarfs*. The bank even loaned the company money to build Disneyland.

A group of local Florida banks also participated in this credit line, contributing $9 million of the $50 million.[37] Another way Disney funded the project was through a common stock issue in 1971.

To pay for the infrastructure throughout the property—such as roads, sewer systems, and water lines—the Reedy Creek Improvement District sold federally subsidized tax-exempt municipal bonds.[38]

With the funding set up, the next major decision dealt with the location for the theme park.

Walt thought the park should be at the back of the property. Afterall, it was going to be the primary thing to lure people in to see his city of tomorrow.[39]

If the park was in the back, visitors would have to traipse through everything in front of it, ensuring they saw the full scope of what Walt had developed.

PRELIMINARY OFFICIAL STATEMENT DATED DECEMBER 12, 1968

OFFICIAL STATEMENT

In the opinion of bond counsel, interest on the Bonds is exempt from all present Federal income taxes under existing statutes and court decisions.

$7,760,000

Reedy Creek Improvement District
Florida

DRAINAGE REVENUE BONDS, SERIES A

Payable solely from and secured by a prior lien upon and pledge of the net revenues derived from the services and facilities of drainage, reclamation and water control improvements acquired and constructed in or on behalf of Subdistrict 1 of the Reedy Creek Improvement District. The District has entered into service contracts with Walt Disney World Co. The aggregate service charges to be paid to the District by Walt Disney World Co. are designed to be sufficient to meet operation and maintenance costs of the drainage, reclamation and water control improvements to be financed by the Series A Bonds and principal and interest charges on the Series A Bonds. Walt Disney Productions, Burbank, California, has guaranteed the payment of such service charges by Walt Disney World Co. until such time as Walt Disney World Co. meets a required earnings level.

Dated: October 1, 1968   Due: October 1, 1970 to 1999, inclusive

Issuable as coupon bonds in the denomination of $5,000 each, registrable as to principal only or as to both principal and interest, and interchangeable as provided in the Bond Resolution. Semi-annual interest (April 1 and October 1) and principal payable at _____ Orlando, Florida, or at the option of the holder at Bankers Trust Company, New York, New York. First interest payment date April 1, 1969. The Bonds are subject to redemption prior to maturity as described herein.

AMOUNTS, MATURITIES, RATES AND YIELDS OR PRICES

(accrued interest from October 1, 1968 to be added)

Amount	Due	Rate	Price or Yield	Amount	Due	Rate	Price or Yield
$100,000	1970	%		$235,000	1985(1)	%	
105,000	1971			250,000	1986(1)		
110,000	1972			265,000	1987(1)		
115,000	1973			280,000	1988(1)		
125,000	1974			295,000	1989(1)		
130,000	1975			315,000	1990(1)		
140,000	1976			335,000	1991(1)		
150,000	1977			355,000	1992(1)		
155,000	1978			375,000	1993(1)		
165,000	1979(1)			400,000	1994(1)		
175,000	1980(1)			420,000	1995(1)		
185,000	1981(1)			445,000	1996(1)		
200,000	1982(1)			475,000	1997(1)		
210,000	1983(1)			500,000	1998(1)		
220,000	1984(1)			530,000	1999(1)		

(1) callable beginning October 1, 1978; see call features herein.

The Bonds are offered when, as and if issued, and received by the Underwriters, subject to prior sale, to withdrawal or modification of the offer without notice, to change in price, and to the approval of legality by Messrs. Bryant, Freeman, Richardson and Watson, Jacksonville, Florida, bond counsel to the District. The Bonds were validated by a decree of the Circuit Court of Osceola County, Florida, on June 14, 1968, which decree was affirmed by the Supreme Court of Florida on November 27, 1968.

New York
20 EXCHANGE PLACE
770-7621
Teletype 212-571-0936

Boston
75 FEDERAL STREET
LI 2-6200
Teletype 617-451-3548

Philadelphia
123 SOUTH BROAD ST.
KI 5-1600
Teletype 215-569-8952

Chicago
33 SOUTH CLARK ST.
AN 3-7350
Teletype 312-222-0706

Los Angeles
OCCIDENTAL CENTER
OLIVE at 12th STREET
746-0920
Teletype 213-683-0388

San Francisco
100 BUSH STREET
EX 7-4900
Teletype 415-393-7811

Dallas
FIRST NAT'L BANK BLDG.
1401 ELM STREET
RI 8-0911

Atlanta
55 MARIETTA STREET
577-3300

Kidder, Peabody & Co. INCORPORATED

FOUNDED 1865

Members of New York Stock Exchange, American Stock Exchange, Boston Stock Exchange, Midwest Stock Exchange, Pacific Coast Stock Exchange and Philadelphia-Baltimore-Washington Stock Exchange.

ALBANY ALTOONA BALTIMORE CHAMBERSBURG DETROIT HARRISBURG LANCASTER LOWELL
MILWAUKEE MINNEAPOLIS NEWARK NEW BEDFORD NEWPORT PORTLAND PROVIDENCE READING
SCRANTON SEATTLE SPOKANE SPRINGFIELD TAUNTON WHITE PLAINS WILKES-BARRE WORCESTER

The date of this Official Statement is _____ , 1968.

Disney's financial executives, the group of men Roy dealt with closely for years, wanted to put the park at the front of the property. There, it would be closest to the highways, and it would get the most exposure from passersby.

This would also be the cheapest option. If it was up front, Disney wouldn't need to clear as much land and create the necessary infrastructure throughout the entire property right off the bat.

Roy didn't think the cheapest option was the best option. He stuck with his brother's idea.[40]

Roy also kept Walt's idea to utilize the concept and layout from Disneyland for Walt Disney World's Magic Kingdom.

Roy went back to Marvin Davis, who had created the master plan for Disneyland in the 1950s. Davis and Dick Irvine utilized what was physically created at Disneyland as their schematic for Florida, except they made everything much larger.

Magic Kingdom utilizes the hub-and-spoke concept just as Disneyland does. At the center of the hub is a much larger and grander castle.

Then radiating out from the castle are the spokes, which lead to the different themed lands.

As the layout and location for the theme park came together, Disney started to move a lot of dirt and water. Roughly 2,500 acres were cleared just for theme park area development.[41]

During an interview with *National Wildlife* magazine, General Joe Potter explained how some of this work was done:

I don't need to tell you about Walt Disney's love of nature and animals. One of the things essential to him was to make our property usable without interfering with the natural growth of trees, plants and wildlife.

The history of Florida is a history of over drainage, but we have developed probably the most complete and sophisticated plan of water reclamation on the largest piece of property in the United

States. This program enables us to control flooding while at the same time preserving the normal water table.

We can now move flood waters off the upper property and down into the lower swamp. We then release the water gradually so as not to harm the area below our property, but quickly enough so as not to disturb the natural plant and animal life or the ecology of the swamp area.[42]

Water from a ninety-nine-square-mile area north of Disney drains onto its property at eleven different points.[43]

To maintain groundwater levels, and keep other parts of the property from being inundated with water, the water control system uses fifty miles of canals, twenty-two miles of levees, and twenty-four water-control structures.[44]

Double-ballasted, nonpowered control gates counteract Florida's typical drought-flood cycle throughout the year.

They automatically float open when water reaches a peak level and automatically close when the high water subsides.

Additionally, thousands of acres are used as a holding basin where the water levels are kept consistent to preserve the flora and fauna.[45]

Great attention to detail was given to the various streams and swamps throughout the property. As Disney initially worked to clean up and manage these areas, the company was informed by conservationists that if it removed the large amounts of rotting logs found in and around the property's swamps, it could potentially kill the alligators and turtles that perch on them.

These critters perch on the logs to dry out the fungus on their feet. The logs needed to stay. Disney removed the ones in bad shape and replaced them with new logs to make sure this ecosystem remained intact.

As part of Walt Disney World's master plan for land conservation, of the over forty square miles of property, nearly one-third has been set aside as a dedicated wildlife conservation area—as of today, there is another third of the property that remains completely undeveloped.[46]

From water control to water cleaning, Disney next moved on to dredging an existing body of water that it wanted to showcase: Bay Lake.

Workers drained three-and-a-half-billion gallons of water from the 450-acre lake. When it was dry, an eight-foot layer of muck was removed from the lake bed. Beneath this mess was pure white sand.

The sand was removed and spread around the 3.8-mile perimeter of the lake to create 80-to-100-foot-wide beaches.[47]

Once that was complete, the lake was refilled (which took six months) and was stocked with 70,000 fingerling bass.

Next, Disney created another body of water, the Seven Seas Lagoon, which is 200 acres large, nearly a mile square, and has a depth of about ten feet.[48]

To carve out the lagoon, over eight million cubic yards of earth were moved—it was considered the biggest earth moving operation since the Hoover Dam—along with the clearing of 1,500 trees. Many of these trees were either replanted around Disney property or used to help to bolster its one-hundred-acre tree farm.

This manmade lagoon was then connected with Bay Lake via a concrete water bridge (navigable aqueduct), which spans a roadway. The bridge allows boats to seamlessly navigate from one body of water to the next.

Underneath the bridge, vehicles coming or going to the area around Magic Kingdom don't even realize there are thousands of gallons of water directly above them.

Creating the Seven Seas Lagoon fulfilled a few needs for the project. First, like a page out of the E.P.C.O.T. playbook, your automobile won't get you to the front gates of Magic Kingdom.

Disney controls access to the theme park. For most visitors, unless they're spending the night at a Disney resort, a trip to the Transportation and Ticket Center (TTC) is required to visit the park.

The TTC is a transportation hub across from Magic Kingdom on the shores of the Seven Seas Lagoon. Here, guests can board a boat (which traverses the lagoon) for their arrival to the park; other transportation options are also available, such as the futuristic, electric-powered monorail.

Second, the millions of cubic yards of dirt excavated to create the lagoon—as many as 60,000 cubic yards of earth, or about 200 truckloads, were being moved in a single sixteen-hour workday—were needed to bolster the Magic Kingdom's foundation.[49]

Hundreds of borings and soil tests revealed the water table to be just four feet below the surface where Magic Kingdom was being built. This would make it difficult to dig deep and structurally support the buildings.

Disney took the fill from the lagoon and raised the entire area for the park by over fourteen feet, thus allowing it to build safely on the land.

By elevating the land, it also gave the architectural and landscape designers a varied area to work with, as the land was naturally flat and not aesthetically pleasing.

General Potter then stepped in and implemented an idea he had used while in the military:

I think I brought the idea of utilidors to this outfit. Normally, in a development, you bury the utilities, and then, when you want to dig to repair a sewer line, you dig up the telephone line too.

Up in Alaska we had utilidors all over the place. A utilidor is a ditch or tunnel in which your utilities go and early in the game I employed three consultants to give us advice on what they thought we should do with the utilities, and one of the things they recommended, which I also recommended was the use of utilidors.[50]

THE UTILIDORS

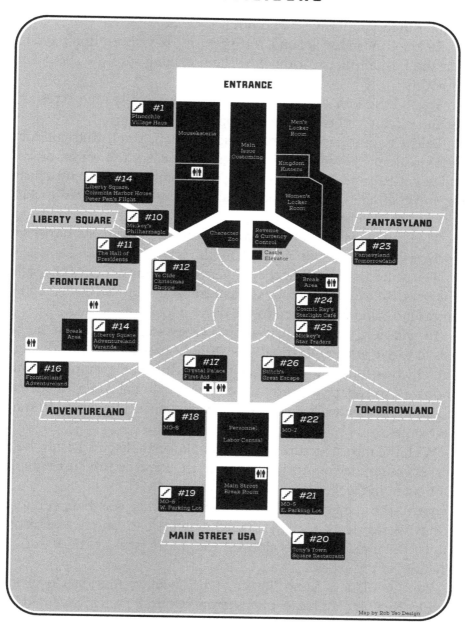

Map by Rob Yeo Design

Disney created a series of these utility corridors, or utilidors, at ground level and then built the park on top of them, which makes Magic Kingdom on the second floor.

As they meander around the park, most visitors don't realize that there is another world below them making sure the show runs smoothly.

Magic Kingdom's utilidor system covers roughly nine acres and has more than a mile of crisscrossing corridors.

Below ground, as the General mentioned, you'll find conduits running along the walls and ceilings. They carry the water, power, and telephone and cable lines, along with compressed air and a heating and cooling system—basically, all of the utilities needed to support and run the theme park above.

This is why when a utility problem arises, park guests rarely see workers fixing the issues above ground.

The utilidors also allow for deliveries to be made out of the sight of guests. Deliveries are made to a centralized location, brought "underground," and distributed to the desired locations above.

In addition, the utilidors allow Disney's costumed cast members to arrive at their destinations without passing through themed lands inconsistent with what they're wearing. For example, people who work in Liberty Square, which has a colonial America theme, shouldn't be seen walking through Fantasyland on their way to start their shifts.

With the infrastructure and master plan established, Disney held a press conference on April 30, 1969, at the Ramada Inn, just outside of Orlando in Ocoee.

Here, the public received a glimpse of what was happening at Disney World. They learned about the theme park and future resort hotels. Disney collectively dubbed the entire project the Vacation Kingdom of the World.

Roy O. Disney, Donn Tatum, Card Walker, Florida Governor Claude Kirk Jr., and executives from United States Steel, RCA,

Monsanto Company, and Aerojet-General Corporation—all of which were sponsors—spoke at the press conference.

Here is a bit of information from the news release, "Vast Walt Disney World Site To Become The 'Vacation Kingdom Of The World'":

Calling upon an array of visual arts—motion picture film, working models and artists renderings—as well as onsite tours of construction progress, officials of Walt Disney World today unveiled plans for a vast new "Vacation Kingdom," to be located on site sixteen miles southwest of Orlando, Florida.

The entire "Vacation Kingdom" will be constructed around a man-made lagoon and natural lake, near which will be located the new "Magic Kingdom" amusement theme park similar to California's Disneyland, five related resort hotels, and an entrance complex.

All in all, this vast destination vacationland—2,500 acres, including some 450 acres of waterways and beaches, have been master planned for resort and recreation—will reach nearly three miles across Walt Disney World from east to west and almost two miles from north and south. With the first facilities to open to the public in October 1971.

The resort hotels will vary in size from 500 to 700 rooms and will be themed along Contemporary, Polynesian, Asian, Venetian and Persian motifs. These will be constructed before and during the first five years of operation.

A transportation network—monorail, watercraft, and land vehicles—will link the attractions with complete facilities for outdoor recreation and entertainment on both land and water.[51]

Further details were provided about Magic Kingdom during the press conference, such as the attractions within each themed land.

Additionally, a few more corporate partnerships—most notably United States Steel—were announced. An agreement was reached for the steel company to build the first two hotels on the property.

According to Edwin H. Gott, chairman of the board of United States Steel, "The 10-story Contemporary A-frame designed hotel and the 12-story Polynesian style resort hotel will be a demonstration of the kind of technical innovation Walt Disney sought to encourage on the part of American industry."[52]

Another corporate partnership was also announced, bringing Disney and the RCA corporation together. RCA created a system specifically for Walt Disney World called WEDCOMM, or the Walter E. Disney Communications Oriented Monitoring and Management System. This system linked computers, telephones, automatic monitoring and control devices, mobile communications, and television together.

On the labor front, Disney revealed a three-year project agreement with the J. B. Allen Contracting Company who would be the general contractor. Additionally, agreements with seventeen individual international and local unions were signed.

Disney hoped to eliminate the possibility of strikes, picketing, or lockouts with its labor forces. A binding arbitrary system, in which grievances and misunderstandings could be handled quickly, was implemented.[53]

As the project headed into 1970 and construction ramped up, J. B. Allen oversaw 10,000 workers and 87 different subcontractors in what was the largest private construction project in the country.[54]

Unfortunately, J. B. Allen started to encounter a few problems, primarily from some of the construction managers.

One manager padded the books with enough hours for sixty additional workers. He would submit imaginary employees' hours for payment and then keep the paychecks for himself.[55]

Another brazen manager stole entire truckloads of building materials. The truck entered the property at the north gate and kept driving through to the south gate.[56] It then drove off of the property and to a housing project the manager was operating on the side a few miles away. [57]

From tools, to showerheads, to televisions—you name it—Disney saw costs skyrocket due to theft. There is a funny story about the televisions, though.

Around Orlando, TV repair shops (yes, hard to believe today that there was such a thing as a television repair shop) saw a surge in people bringing in the same model of television to be fixed.

Disney's TVs wouldn't work off of its property. Each television was linked and programmed for Disney's own network and programming.

Not knowing this, the workers often stole the TVs. Back at home when they turned on their pilfered televisions, they were useless. So off to the repair shops they went, figuring their sets were broken, never realizing they were locked when outside of Disney's network.[58]

Each of these situations led to cost overruns and pushed the project off schedule, which didn't make Roy happy.

By October of 1970, with just under a year until opening day, Roy called a meeting with the general contractor. He wanted to know how the project was progressing and what problems it was having.

A few days before the meeting, he made a phone call to Disneyland. He wanted Disney's director of finance, Carl Bongirno, to come down and sit in on the meeting with J. B. Allen. Believe it or not, Carl actually got his start with Disney back in Colorado at Disney's Celebrity Sports Center.

Here's how Carl remembers the meeting with the general contractor:

About a year before Walt Disney World opened, in October of 1970, I got this call from Roy, who said "Carl we are having a big powwow down in Florida. I want you there. I am very concerned about the construction management company team we have down there. I want to get to the bottom of this.

If we aren't going to open this theme park on October 1st, 1971, we are going to bankrupt this company. We have got commitments to participants, bankers and stockholders. I am concerned that things aren't going too well."

I was down there for the meeting. It was held in a doublewide trailer. We must have had 50 guys in that room made up of our general contractor at the time, J. B. Allen, who was also involved in the building of Disneyland, and all of our people: Roy O. Disney, Donn Tatum, Card Walker, Dick Nunis, myself and Joe Fowler.

Roy had J. B. Allen give a presentation with Joe Fowler on the situation on the site and how things were going and problems that they were having and so-forth and so-on. It was a fairly lengthy meeting—a couple hours.

At the end of the meeting Roy said, "J. B. Allen that was very good. Thank you very much for a very detailed analysis and briefing. I appreciate it very much. I just have one question and I want a truthful answer. Will this project open on October 1st, 1971?"

As people were responding nonverbally, Roy is looking around the room. All the J. B. Allen guys are shaking their heads no, back and forth, left to right.

All the Disney guys are shaking their heads yes. We were brought up that if you have an objective you accomplish it. Will we open? Yes, we will open. I don't know what we are going to have to do but we are going to open.

The J. B. Allen guys are saying no. Roy Disney—I was sitting a couple seats away from him—turns beet red. Beet red. I mean all of the blood in his body rushed to his head.

He jolts up onto his feet and pounds the table. He says "Goddam. Son of a bitch. The life of our company is at stake and you people from J. B. Allen are telling me that you can't open this project on October 1st, 1971, after a two hour presentation. I can't believe this!" He went on a tirade for a minute or so. Then he stormed out of the trailer and slammed the door. I thought it was going to come off its hinges.

I was staying at the company cottages. Roy was in one, Card Walker was in one, Donn Tatum was in one, and I was in one. About two hours later I got a call from Card. He said "Carl, I'm glad I caught you. Why don't you come over." So I went over to his cottage, which I think was next door or two doors over.

He started by saying he had just finished a meeting with Roy. Roy was extremely upset and he made the decision to kick J. B. Allen off the project. We are going to run it ourselves.

He said "I'm sure glad you're here in Florida to be Joe Fowler's number two guy." [Laughs] I was on a business trip. I was intending to eventually move to Florida but not for about a year.

So I didn't say anything. I think Card thought I was already located in Florida. He knew I was there, but he didn't know that I hadn't moved yet.

He said "I want you and Phil Smith to sit down with J. B. Allen and negotiate their departure. And then work with Joe Fowler in getting this place open on time."[59]

After his meeting with Card, Carl went back to his cottage and called his wife. He told her he was living in Florida now and she should put their house up for sale the next day, then join him as soon as she could.

Phil Smith and Carl relieved J. B. Allen of its responsibility at Walt Disney World. And just like that, Disney was in the construction business. It formed the Buena Vista Construction company and now controlled its own destiny.

Despite the slowdown and issues with its contractors, Walt Disney World was able to open its first building to the public on January 10, 1970.[60] The Preview Center for the Vacation Kingdom was on the edge of the property near Interstate 4 and State Road 535.

Visitors to the center saw a huge model of the resort, could watch a short film about the Vacation Kingdom, and were able to acquaint themselves with everything that was set to open in under two years.

The center was staffed with information hostesses (rumor had it they kept track of license plates, particularly those from out of state, for research purposes[61]), had a snack bar, and of course, sold Disney merchandise. There was even a temporary post office set up so visitors could send out a Walt Disney World post card.[62]

This on-site presence stimulated interest from prospective customers and potential employees. In the year leading up to the opening, there were, on average, 1,800 in-person inquiries about employment at Walt Disney World each week. Another 8,000 came via mail every month.

When it was all said and done, of the 120,000 job applicants, 35,000 people were interviewed and about 5,000 were hired to staff the Vacation Kingdom.[63]

The Preview Center was a very effective way to introduce the public to Walt Disney World. While the center was open, $11 million dollars' worth of tickets to Magic Kingdom park were presold and thousands of reservations for the two hotels were booked.[64]

Speaking of those on-site hotels, these were Disney's first foray into the hotel business. Back at Disneyland, the company did not own or operate the Disneyland Hotel.

To help Disney learn the hotel business, it leased the Hilton Inn South in Orlando. The hotel was operating and active, but it shut

382812 RECORDED   DEC 28 2 10 PM '70   O.R. 2016 PG 24

FLORIDA 1963 LAWS
FS 84.131

NOTICE OF COMMENCEMENT

(PREPARE IN DUPLICATE)

RAMCO FORM 408

State of Florida   }
County of

The undersigned hereby informs all concerned that improvements will be made to certain real property, and in accordance with section 84.131 of the Florida Statutes, the following information is stated in this NOTICE OF COMMENCEMENT.

Description of property...................(Attached)

General description of improvements...........Peter Pan Facility and Ride

Owner..............7...WALT DISNEY WORLD CO.

Address..............P.O. Box 40, Orlando, Florida 32802

Owner's interest in site of the improvement..........Fee Simple

Fee Simple Title holder (if other than owner)

Name..............

Address..............

Contractor..............Buena Vista Construction Co.

Address..............P.O. Box 40, Orlando, Florida 32802

Surety (if any)..............None

Address..............Amount of bond $ None

Name of person within the State of Florida designated by owner upon whom notices or other documents may be served.

Name..............Philip N. Smith

Address..............P.O. Box 40, Orlando, Florida 32802

In addition to himself, owner designates the following person to receive a copy of the Lienor's Notice as provided in Section 84.061 [2] [b], Florida Statutes. (Fill in at Owner's option).

Name..............W. F. Pennell, Jr.

Address..............P.O. Box 40, Orlando, Florida 32802

THIS SPACE FOR RECORDER'S USE ONLY

WALT DISNEY WORLD CO.

Secretary
Owner

Sworn to and subscribed before me this

23rd day of December 19 70

Notary Public

FLORIDA 1963 LAWS   FS 84.131   272247 RECORDED   RAMCO FORM 400

JUN 25   9 50 AM 1969

rec 1846 PG 910

Notice of Commencement

(PREPARE IN DUPLICATE)

To whom it may concern:

The undersigned hereby informs you that improvements will be made to certain real property, and in accordance with section 84.131 of the Florida Statutes, the following information is stated in this NOTICE OF COMMENCEMENT.

Description of property   Attached

General description of improvements   Construction of Haunted Mansion and Small World Facility Buildings, WALT DISNEY WORLD

Owner   Walt Disney World Co.

Address   P. O. Box 40, Orlando, Florida 32802

Owner's interest in site of the improvement   Fee Simple

Fee Simple Title holder (if other than owner)

Name

Address

Contractor   Allen Contracting Co., Inc.

Address   P. O. Box 38, Orlando, Florida 32802

Surety (if any)   None

Address   N/A   Amount of bond $ None

Name of person within the State of Florida designated by owner upon whom notices or other documents may be served:

Name   Phillip N. Smith

Address   P. O. Box 40, Orlando, Florida 32802

In addition to himself, owner designates the following person to receive a copy of the Lienor's Notice as provided in Section 84.061 (2) (b), Florida Statutes. (Fill in at Owner's option).

Name   W. D. Ellermeier

Address   P. O. Box 38, Orlando, Florida 32802

THIS SPACE FOR RECORDER'S USE ONLY

Walt Disney World Co.

By _____

Title   Asst. Secretary

Sworn to and subscribed before me this

24th   day of   June   19 69

_____

Notary Public

Notary Public, State of Florida at Large

My Commission Expires Feb. 18, 1973

Bonded by American Fire & Casualty Co.

down for a brief period so the owners could transition to having Disney run the show.

The hotel reopened under Disney control in May of 1970. Disney employees underwent training at the Hilton, learning the hospitality industry in and out while they waited for their future places of employment to open, the Contemporary Resort Hotel and the Polynesian Village Resort.

Both of Disney's on-site hotels were developed by the architecture firm Welton Becket and Disney's inhouse creative division, the previously mentioned WED Enterprises Inc.

The two firms worked together and developed the specs for a modular hotel room concept. Next, they invited a few industrial firms to develop a concept and system to be used at Walt Disney World.

As discussed, Disney had agreed to partner with United States Steel, who devised the modular system, a system that, in theory, should have expedited the whole construction process.

US Steel paid between $50 to $60 million to build the Contemporary Resort Hotel and the Polynesian Village Resort on Disney's property. It would own the buildings, but Disney would retain ownership of the land they occupied. Disney would then lease and operate the resorts from US Steel.

The design for the Polynesian, and the Contemporary, changed a bit from what had been announced in April of 1969. The Polynesian went more horizontal than vertical—it had a village-style layout, rather than being a twelve-story tower.

The Contemporary became a fourteen story A-frame structure with rooms terraced up both sides of the A. A very futuristic concept, the monorail passes right though the interior of the hotel—the theme of the resort also aligns with Magic Kingdom's Tomorrowland.

The structure itself is 184-feet high, 220-feet wide at its base, and 468-feet long, and it contains 1.4 million square feet of space. Some of that space—specifically the Ballroom of the Americas—was used by President Nixon on November 17, 1973, when he claimed he was "not a crook."

To follow through with the newly devised modular construction concept, US Steel set up a factory about three miles from where the hotels were being built. At the factory, each hotel room was constructed. The rooms are fifteen-feet wide, nine-feet high and thirty-feet long.

All of the interior elements for the room—utilities, lights, bathroom fixtures, you name it—were completed at the factory and then trucked over to the hotel.

Once on site, the rooms were hoisted into place; the electrical and plumbing connections had already been prefabricated and included in each one. The process should have been easy peasy—it often wasn't.

This format was supposed to expedite the process and allow US Steel to place seven to ten rooms into the hotel structure per day. And no, contrary to urban legend, they weren't made to be popped out again for refurbishment—once the rooms were in, they were in.

After the first few rooms went into place, which in and of itself wasn't as easy as they had expected, workers had to stagger and alternate where the rooms went into the A-frame.

If they put them all into one side first, they would strain the structure of the hotel. So they needed to put up two cranes, one on each side of the hotel, and alternate sides as they inserted the rooms into the structure.[65]

Turned out "unitized modular construction," as it was called, seemed much easier on paper, at least for the Contemporary Resort, as it was a high-rise. Sliding the completed rooms into the Polynesian resort was a much easier task.

While there were legitimate logistical and technical problems that hindered the project, the relationship between US Steel and Disney started to strain during construction.

From the start of the erection of the steel frame to opening day, they had only eleven months to complete the Contemporary. Things were moving too slowly and there was doubt as to whether this project was going to be completed in time for opening day.

Frustrated and aggravated with the situation—much like what had happened with J. B. Allen—Roy eventually negotiated a buyout of US Steel.[66]

MODULAR HOUSING

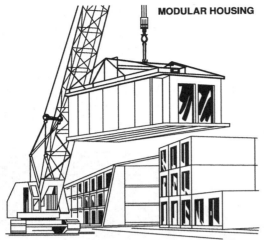

One of Disney World's innovations is the hotel which is located near the theme park. Every one of the hotel's self-contained, lightweight, family-size living units is built completely off-site and hoisted into place by crane in an experiment to cut the high cost of housing.

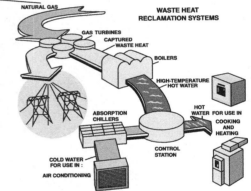

WASTE HEAT RECLAMATION SYSTEMS

NATURAL GAS

GAS TURBINES

CAPTURED WASTE HEAT

BOILERS

HIGH-TEMPERATURE HOT WATER

HOT WATER FOR USE IN COOKING AND HEATING

ABSORPTION CHILLERS

CONTROL STATION

COLD WATER FOR USE IN :

AIR CONDITIONING

Two jet fighter engines run on cleanburning natural gas to produce most of Disney World's electricity. Energy from the waste heat is captured and passed through boilers, heating water is used for cooking and heating of buildings. A chemical process derives cold water for air conditioning.

UNDERGROUND UTILITY CORRIDOR

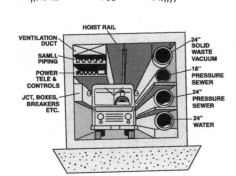

GROUND LEVEL

HOIST RAIL

VENTILATION DUCT

SAMLL PIPING

POWER TELE & CONTROLS

JCT, BOXES, BREAKERS ETC.

24" SOLID WASTE VACUUM

18" PRESSURE SEWER

24" PRESSURE SEWER

24" WATER

Cross section of underground utilidor shows separate storm sewage. Clean water from roofs and amusement rides runs into Bay Lake, oily runoff water from parking lots goes into holding ponds for treatment.

As 1971 soldiered on, behind the scenes, people were privately starting to doubt if not only the hotels, but the project in general, would be ready by October 1. Perhaps J. B. Allen had been right.

In late May and early June of 1971, Dick Nunis visited the construction site. At the time, he was working at Disneyland.

Nunis was someone who was very familiar with the "Disney way" of getting things done. After seeing the state of the future Vacation Kingdom, he was asked by Card Walker and Donn Tatum if he thought the project could open by October 1.

His reply was, no, not under the present circumstances. When pushed for what he thought needed to be done to get to the finish line, he said the only way it was going to happen is if all of the resources of the company were thrown into it.[67]

The following week, Nunis was transferred from Disneyland to Disney World. He was told not to worry about budgets and that whomever he needed in Florida would immediately be sent there.

As Dick was quoted:

From then on, we literally stripped the other divisions. The Studio. Design. Disneyland. They began to call us the "Nunis Raiders."

We had a couple hundred key management people and experts on the site now. There was no discussions of changing the date. We had to open. I carried a tape recorder and dictated all day long as I went around the project. Secretaries typed the memos at night and sent them out the next day.[68]

Things seemed to be progressing nicely under General Nunis—he hung a caricature of himself dressed as General Patton in his office.[69]

Local magazine *Orlando-Land* gave an exclusive report from a shop supervisor about the buzz of activity taking place night and day at Walt Disney World.

Here is every minute detail in order of execution, thought out and planned by those anonymous WED "imagineers" 3,000 miles across the continent, many of whom have never even seen Florida.

Along one wall of the office is a file of project blueprints sent east from California. One set for Cinderella Castle, one for the Railroad station and so on. For some projects, exquisite scale models have been put together by WED.

"As soon as we get the authorization, we set up a job board for a project and go to work," Bud Washo says. "We have complete material takeoff. We decide what will work best. We're always researching new materials. We've never been given anything we couldn't make. This department ends up with the most miscellaneous group of things you could imagine. We're making ancient stone for the Cinderella Castle, coral rock and shipwrecks for the submarine ride, animal hides, boat canopies . . . oh well, you name it."

What it amounts to is, first, building solid steel and concrete structures (strong enough to resist hurricanes) and then applying exterior and interior "costumes" that turn basic buildings into a town hall or a colonial tavern or a south seas ceremonial house or ancient Asian ruins. Then installing the marvelous Audio-Animatronic figures from California (for the shows).

Then planting masses of trees and shrubs and flowers appropriate to the theme of each area. Add locomotives from the Yucatan, monorails from Orlando's Martin Marietta plant, boats from Tampa Bay, a skyride from Switzerland, a carousel from New Jersey and this and that from everywhere.

Sprinkle liberally with Disney men and women in costumes to match the "costumes" on the building. And you have Walt Disney World.[70]

Well, there you have it, bibbidi-bobbidi-boo. If only creation and construction were just that simple. That blurb makes it all sound a bit too simplistic, especially when considering the logistics and amount of innovation that was put into the project.

Disney went the extra mile for authenticity, literally—it brought in components from around the world for its make-believe world.

Landscape architects imported trees from Africa, Japan, and New Zealand, not to mention California and Texas. By opening day, nearly 60,000 trees and shrubs of some 800 varieties had been planted, along with enough sod to cover the equivalent of 500 football fields.

Liberty Square received the largest tree on the property when a live oak weighing thirty-five tons was transplanted there.[71] For a bit more authenticity, the large rocks needed for this colonial themed land were obtained directly from the area where Washington had crossed the Delaware.

The concrete beams needed for the monorail—all 337 of them—ranging in length from 85 feet to 110 feet, were assembled and trucked in from Tacoma, Washington.[72]

Another west coast acquisition was the 160 Grand Prix race cars for Disney's Grand Prix Raceway. These were brought in from Mountain View, California.

The list of out-of-state acquisitions could go on and on: wigs for animatronics from Guatemala, gas turbines from Toronto, industrial-sized boilers from Houston, Texas.

However, it wasn't always about purchasing the items. Oftentimes, Disney needed to develop and produce them in-house. For example, the "it's a small world" attraction required 1,637 handmade figures, which Disney made in California.[73]

For the Country Bear Jamboree, sculptors used nine tons of clay to make life-size representations of each one of the twenty bears in the show before crafting the audio-animatronic versions.[74]

In creating the Hall of Presidents, two full-time research librarians devoted eighteen months to providing writers, designers and painters with more than 600 books, 300 magazines, and 5,000 photographs as references to accurately create and portray the past leaders of the country.[75]

Special paint colors were even developed and painted throughout Main Street so when it's photographed the memories caught on film seem as vibrant as when the street is viewed in person.

The buildings on Main Street were also specially constructed. Utilizing an old movie set building trick, structures appear to be taller than they actually are through an illusion of forced perspective.

Here's how it works: by reducing the scale of a building as it grows taller and taller—with the second floor smaller than the first and the third floor smaller than the second—the building is given an appearance of being farther away.

For example, on Main Street, the Plaza Ice Cream Parlor has a first-story height of twelve feet; the second story is ten feet tall, and the third story is eight feet tall. This technique is also used on Cinderella Castle.

This attention to detail and extra effort to make Walt Disney World unique didn't stop with the things seen throughout the theme park; it extended into the behind-the-scenes infrastructure as well.

According to an interview with General Potter from 1984, much of this innovation could not have happened without the control they wield through the Reedy Creek Improvement District:

> It gave us all the powers of the two counties in which we sit to the exclusion of their exercising any powers, and of course it let us issue bonds. We could do anything the city or the county could do. The only powers that still reside on us from outside are the taxing power of Orange County, the sales tax of the state and the inspection of elevators.
>
> We had to have the power of our own building codes. We adopted the [Southeast's strongest] building codes, which still exist in the Reedy Creek Improvement District. We had to do our own zoning. The zoning of a property is a very political thing.[76]

Just because Disney had this freedom and control didn't mean it cut corners or took an easier or cheaper route to construction. In fact, it tended to go the more expensive and time-consuming course.

For example, it was uncommon in the 1960s to have a fire sprinkler in every room of a building. Disney's property featured sprinklers, smoke detectors, and fire monitoring systems in every room on its property.[77]

Disney also pioneered and developed strict standards for structural design and implemented the use of new materials, such as fiberglass, which was often used for rides and show buildings.

When it came to utilities and how to power the property, everything was built from the ground up. This was done in part so the resort wouldn't have to draw power from the nearby counties of Orange and Osceola. It was also done in a way to minimally impact the environment.

Disney installed two 8,000 horsepower fighter jet engines that run on clean-burning natural gas. The engines push a stream of 1,500-degree air through turbines geared to electronic generators.

Normally, the waste heat from a process like this would be discharged into a nearby body of water, potentially affecting the ecosystem through thermal pollution. Disney, however, captures this heated water and sends it through boilers that take the temperature to over 400 degrees.

The energy from this hot water is then utilized in a lithium bromide chemical process to chill down the water for air-conditioning, which is used throughout the property. The water is also piped into faucets and spigots in the park.[78]

To handle sewage and waste, a $2.5 million activated sludge sewage plant cleans 3.3 million gallons of water per day in three stages. This produces an effluent that nearly meets public health drinking water standards. The sludge removed during this process is used as a soil conditioner and fertilizer.[79]

In terms of solid waste and garbage, Disney installed the country's first automatic waste disposal system, called the Automated Vacuum Assisted Collection, or AVAC.

Developed in Sweden, the system features a large network of collection points throughout the theme park. Here, trash is deposited, and then pneumatic tubes whisk it away at close to sixty miles per hour.

The trash collects at one point, is compacted, and is then trucked away to be incinerated. The central compactor automatically signals a computer in Disney's DACS computer room to indicate when the room is full and needs to be tended to.

Located in the utilidors, the Digital Animation Control System, or DACS, kept the Vacation Kingdom running. The hundreds of audio-animatronic characters were orchestrated with this computer system.

At the time, DACS was able to control more than 72,000 individual functions every second. For an attraction such as the Country Bear Jamboree, DACS controlled the voices and gestures of the bears and also operated the lighting, opened the theater doors, and raised and lowered the curtains.[80]

Similar DACS systems were in place to make hotel reservations, chill refrigerators, control air-conditioning, maintain security, coordinate transportation, detect smoke, and track the environment's quality. DACS even handled the music in the hotel lobbies.

This automated technology was revolutionary for the time and resembled what Walt would have hoped to spread throughout his E.P.C.O.T. project.

As opening day approached, though, there was still quite a bit of work DACS couldn't automate. On the eve of the park's debut, it was an all-hands-on deck effort to get the park open. Seventy-eight-year-old Roy O. Disney was even seen helping unload a truck.

Dick Nunis pitched in to lay down the last of the grass in front of the Contemporary Resort Hotel.[81]

And just mere hours before the first guests strolled down Main

Street, a helicopter was flown into Fantasyland to expedite the curing of the concrete, as it was still wet.[82]

As Roy O. Disney promised, and later demanded, four years, nine months, and sixteen days after Walt Disney died, his Magic Kingdom opened on October 1, 1971, and virtually debt free (at the price of nearly $400 million, this could actually be the most exceptional accomplishment of the whole enterprise).

Opening day came and went. It was pretty unremarkable, just the way Disney wanted it.

The news media predicted crowds in the 30,000–35,000 range.[83]

By midday on October 1, Donn Tatum reported a head count of between 2,500 and 2,800 paid customers, remarking, "We're not disappointed by the turnout. It's just what we wanted."[84] By the end of day two, 11,115 guests visited the park.[85]

Disney called the Vacation Kingdom's first month in business a preview month. It didn't want the big crowds—it needed to work out any kinks without a packed house. This was the logic behind opening the park in October, as it's traditionally the slowest tourist time in Florida.

Instead of a ceremony with pomp and circumstance, or a festive ribbon cutting ceremony, Disney decided to hold a Grand Opening Spectacular over a three-day weekend from October 23 to October 25.

It was here that Roy read the park dedication:

Walt Disney World is a tribute to the philosophy and life of Walter Elias Disney . . . and to the talents, the dedication and the loyalty of the entire Disney organization that made Walt Disney's dream come true.

May Walt Disney World bring joy and inspiration and new knowledge to all who come to this happy place . . . a Magic Kingdom where the young at heart of all ages can laugh and play and learn—together.

Dedicated this 25th day of October 1971.

Many of the events from the grand opening celebration were broadcast on television during a ninety-minute special that introduced America to their newest Disney park.

An estimated fifty-two-million people watched that evening on October 29, from 8:00 to 9:30 p.m.

A month after the opening celebration, on November 26, 1971, Walt Disney World had its first attendance record: 55,000 people jammed into the park that day. Officials turned away an additional 3,000 cars.[86] Through January of 1972, just four months after opening day, over two million people visited the Vacation Kingdom.[87]

Roy accomplished his brother's final dream, or at least part of it. Along with the tens of thousands of people who had directly and indirectly worked on the project, he had brought Walt Disney World to life. At the end of the opening day, Roy became nostalgic and reminisced about his life with Walt:

My brother and I went into business together almost a half a century ago. And he really was in my opinion, truly a genius— creative, with great determination and drive; all through his entire life he was never pushed off course or diverted by other things. Walt probably had fewer secrets than any man, cause he was always talking to whoever would listen![88]

Walt had felt the same way about Roy. When he had the opportunity, usually during interviews about their company, Walt let the world know how he felt about his older brother:

I had this brother eight and a half years older. I could go and talk to him and tell him things I could never tell my dad. My father never understood me. He was a wonderful man but very strict. I would tell my dad I was going to be an artist, he couldn't see it. But my big brother would say, "Kid, go ahead!" He said "Kid, I'm for you." He encouraged me. When he was away we wrote letters. I could tell him what I was going to do and he'd write back: "Go ahead, kid. Good for you!"

I was fortunate I had a big brother, And he's still with me. And I still love him. I argue with him. Sometimes I think he's the stubbornest so and so I ever met in my life. I don't know what the hell I'd do without him.[89]

Less than three months after Walt Disney World opened, at the age of seventy-eight, Roy Oliver Disney died from a stroke on December 20, 1971, in the same hospital where his brother had passed away.

Ironically, the two men who helped to bring some of the most popular fairy tales in history to life created quite a fairy tale themselves.

The poor farm boys from the Midwest who started a small family business together in the 1920s left an indelible mark on their world and ours.

Walt and Roy's legacy—the global corporation bearing their last name—is one of the largest family entertainment and media conglomerates in the world. As Walt often said, it's all because of family. "The important thing is the family. If you can keep the family together—and that's the backbone of our whole business, catering to families—that's what we hope to do."[90]

Today, Walt Disney World—and most notably, Magic Kingdom—stands as the world's most visited theme park. Every year, tens of millions of families pay homage to Walt Disney when they visit his parks in central Florida.

Critics of Walt Disney World and its Reedy Creek Improvement District claim Disney basically did a bait and switch. The project was presented one way and the legislation was passed accordingly.

Decades later the company still hasn't achieved what it initially set out to do: create a city of tomorrow. Nor has Disney been able to fully escape comments from its detractors regarding the unprecedented control it wields.

One thing is for sure, though, regardless of how you feel about Disney's quasi-government municipality, the state of Florida made out OK in the deal.

In February of 2016, then Florida Governor Rick Scott said Florida had become the first state in the US to welcome more than 105 million out-of-state and international tourists.

Where was this announcement was made? You guessed it—Walt Disney World. The governor noted that Orlando is critical to the state's success: "Orlando is the most visited destination in the United States. It's the most visited city, and certainly the home of the theme park capital of the world, right? No place else on earth can compare to that." [91]

In 2014, Orlando alone recorded sixty-two million visitors, which includes in-state, out-of-state, and international visitors. I'm sure Governors Burns and Kirk would both marvel at the influx of visitors to Florida, due in large part to Disney.

Walt Disney World's presence drastically changed the landscape of Florida, culturally and economically. Just how much the resort influences central Florida was unfortunately seen in the spring of 2020, when the parks and hotels were shuttered due to the Covid-19 outbreak.

The entire country, and much of the world, suffered. However, central Florida was hit particularly hard when tourism ground to a halt, offering a rare and frightening glimpse of what life is like for the state without Disney.

At its peak the Walt Disney World resort employs more than 70,000 people on site. There are multiple theme parks, hundreds of restaurants, and over twenty-five hotels with tens of thousands of hotel rooms.

With a daily population often swelling to nearly 200,000 people, and with tens of thousands of visitors spending the night—having all of their daily needs fulfilled on site—perhaps Disney World has lived up to some of the expectations set forth in the late 1960s.

Recently, a remnant of Walt's original dream of having residents live on his property also came true.

In 2010, Disney announced it was building a community of homes called Golden Oak, just southeast of Magic Kingdom.

Today, many families reside within Walt's Disney World. I'd be curious to hear his thoughts about the cost to live there—starting prices to live a hop, skip, and a jump away from Magic Kingdom start in the mid-$2 millions and top out in excess of $10 million. This certainly doesn't sound like Progress City, but I'm sure if you can afford it, it's pretty magical.

OPENING DAY

General Admission: adult admission, $3.50; junior admission, ages twelve through seventeen, $2.50; and children three through eleven, $1.00.

If you felt the need to bring man's best friend, your four-legged friend could stay at the Disney kennel for fifty cents a day, which included a lunch.

The cost of individual attractions ranged from ten cents to ninety cents.[1]

There were even two package deals for the grand opening. The Family Fun Vacation package consisted of a three-day-and-two-night stay at one of the hotels, along with admission to the park for three guests and tickets for twenty-one attractions. The rates per person were $61.50 for an adult, $25.00 for a junior, and $23.50 per child. Single occupancy was $100.50.[2]

Then there was the Vacation Kingdom package, offering four days and three nights at one of the hotels, admission to the Magic Kingdom, and tickets for twenty-eight attractions. Rates were $90.00 per adult, $36.50 for a junior, and $35.50 per child. Single occupancy was $148.50.[3]

If a package deal wasn't to your liking, you could spend the night at the Polynesian Village or the Contemporary for $25.00 to $44.00 a night at either hotel. The Fort Wilderness Campsite was $11.00 for trailer sites, including hookup.[4]

REEDY CREEK IMPROVEMENT DISTRICT

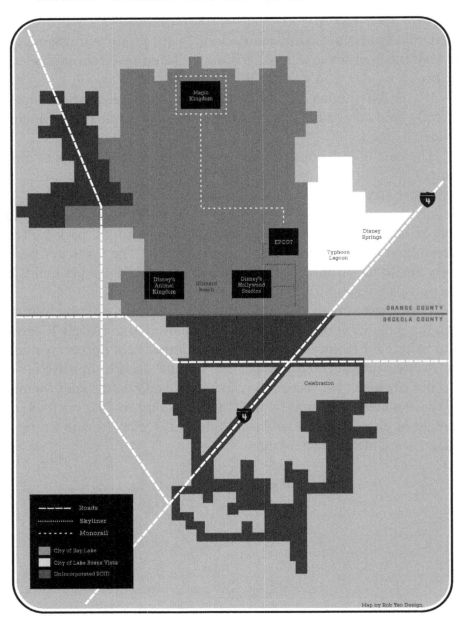

Map by Rob Yeo Design

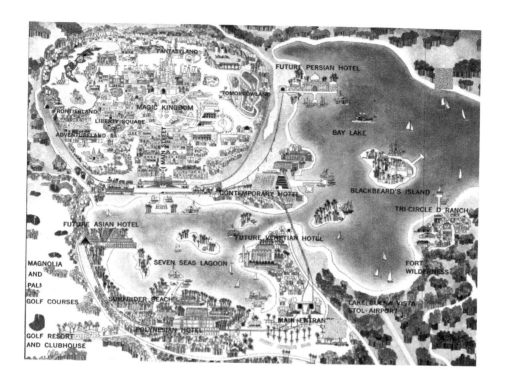

ENDNOTES

Introduction

1. Walt Disney Productions (1971, October). Eyes and Ears of Walt Disney Zehnder, L. E. (1975). Florida's Disney World: Promises and Problems, "The Year of Transition." Tallahassee, FL: Peninsular Pub.
2. Foster, R. (1992). The Founding of a Kingdom. Unpublished manuscript, RCID Walt Disney World Files, Robert Foster, University of Central Florida, Orlando.

Chapter One

1. Worldometer (2020). "Population" (real time world statistics). Retrieved November 16, 2020, from https://www.worldometers.info/.
2. Foglesong, R. E. (2003). *Married to the Mouse: Walt Disney World and Orlando* (p. Xii). New Haven, CT: Yale University Press.
3. Sanchez, J. (1984, February 19). *Orlando Sentinel*, "Town was home to Disney grandparents."
4. Walt Disney Productions (1982). *Walt Disney World: The First Decade* (pp. 9–10). Anaheim, CA: Walt Disney Productions.
5. Smith, D. (2002). *Quotable Walt Disney*. Glendale, CA: Disney Editions.
6. Walt Disney Productions (1982).
7. Smith, D. (2002).
8. Fjellman, S. (1992). *Vinyl Leaves: Walt Disney World and America*. Boulder, CO: Westview Press.
9. Smith, D. (2002).

Chapter Two

1. Koenig, D. (2014). *Realityland: True-Life Adventures at Walt Disney World*, "The Undercover Expansion." Irvine, CA: Bonaventure Press.
2. Smith, D. (2002). *Quotable Walt Disney*. Glendale, CA: Disney Editions.
3. Smith, D. (2002).
4. Sklar, M. (1967, September 21). *Walt Disney World: Background and Philosophy*. Burbank, CA.
5. Sklar, M. (1967, September 21).
6. Walt Disney Family Museum (2014, July 17). "In Walt's Own Words: Plussing Disneyland." Retrieved November 16, 2020, from https://www.waltdisney.org/blog/walts-own-words-plussing-disneyland.
7. Smith, D. (2002).
8. Smith, D. (2002).
9. Foster, R. (1992). *The Founding of a Kingdom*. Unpublished manuscript, RCID Walt Disney World Files, Robert Foster, University of Central Florida, Orlando.

10. Foster, R. (1992).
11. Crockett, C. (2014, March 21). *Priceonomics*, "The Rise and Fall of Professional Bowling." Retrieved November 16, 2020, from https://priceonomics.com/the-rise-and-fall-of-professional-bowling/.
12. Crockett, C. (2014, March 21).
13. Key, H. (1959, December 15). *Rocky Mountain News*, "Jack Benny, Disney Put Celebrity Lanes Show on the Road."
14. Ruttum Senturia, L. (2020, January 25). Denver Public Library, "Celebrity Sports Center: Bowling, Video Games, and Your Very First Water Slide." Retrieved November 16, 2020, from https://history.denverlibrary.org/news/celebrity-sports-center.
15. *Rocky Mountain News* (1962, September 4). *Rocky Mountain News*, "Disney Here for Anniversary of Sports Center."
16. Forsyth, D. (2009, February 04). *Buckfifty*.org, "Celebrity Sports Center, 1960–1994." Retrieved November 16, 2020, from http://buckfifty.org/2009/02/celebrity/.
17. Foster, R. (1992).
18. Foster, R. (1992).
19. Foster, R. (1992).
20. Foster, R. (1992).
21. Foster, R. (1992).
22. Cruz, S. (2014, April 2). *Orange County Register*, "A hand in creating Disneyland."
23. Goldberg, A. H. (2016). *The Disney Story: Chronicling the Man, the Mouse, and the Parks*. Philadelphia, PA: Quaker Scribe Publishing.
24. Goldberg, A. H. (2016).
25. Goldberg, A. H. (2016).

Chapter Three

1. Foster, R. (1992). *The Founding of a Kingdom*. Unpublished manuscript, RCID Walt Disney World Files, Robert Foster, University of Central Florida, Orlando.
2. Foglesong, R. E. (2003). *Married to the Mouse: Walt Disney World and Orlando* (p. Xii). New Haven, CT: Yale University Press.
3. Vagnini, S. (2016, September 28). *D23: The Official Disney Fan Club*, "How Walt Disney World Found Its Home in Florida." Retrieved November 16, 2020, from https://d23.com/we-say-its-disney/.
4. Foster, R. (1992).
5. Foster, R. (1992).
6. Foster, R. (1992).
7. Koenig, D. (2014). *Realityland: True-Life Adventures at Walt Disney World*, "The Undercover Expansion." Irvine, CA: Bonaventure Press.

8. Foster, R. (1992).
9. Foster, R. (1992).
10. Vagnini, S. (2016, September 28).
11. Vagnini, S. (2016, September 28).
12. Zehnder, L. E. (1975). *Florida's Disney World: Promises and Problems,* "The Year of Transition." Tallahassee, FL: Peninsular Pub.
13. Donofrio, C. (2019, August 1). *Realtor.com,* "What Is a Real Estate Option Contract—and Do You Need One to Buy a House?" Retrieved November 16, 2020, https://www.realtor.com/.
14. Foster, R. (1992).

Chapter Four

1. Foster, R. (1992). *The Founding of a Kingdom.* Unpublished manuscript, RCID Walt Disney World Files, Robert Foster, University of Central Florida, Orlando.
2. Foster, R. (1992).
3. Foster, R. (1992).
4. CIA (n.d.). Freedom of Information Act. Retrieved November 16, 2020, from https://www.cia.gov/library/readingroom/document/cia-rdp90-552r000202030048-4.
5. Drinkhall, J. (1980, April 18). *The Wall Street Journal,* "IRS vs. CIA."
6. Foster, R. (1992).
7. Foster, R. (1992).
8. Foster, R. (1992).
9. Foster, R. (1992).
10. Foster, R. (1992).
11. Vagnini, S. (2016, September 28). *D23: The Official Disney Fan Club,* "How Walt Disney World Found Its Home in Florida." Retrieved November 16, 2020, from https://d23.com/we-say-its-disney/.
12. Foster, R. (1992).
13. Foster, R. (1992).
14. Foster, R. (1992).
15. Foster, R. (1992).
16. Foster, R. (1992).
17. Foster, R. (1992).
18. Foster, R. (1992).

Chapter Five

1. Foster, R. (1992). *The Founding of a Kingdom.* Unpublished manuscript, RCID Walt Disney World Files, Robert Foster, University of Central Florida, Orlando.
2. Foster, R. (1992).

3. Foster, R. (1992).
4. Foster, R. (1992).
5. Foster, R. (1992).
6. Foglesong, R. E. (2003). *Married to the Mouse: Walt Disney World and Orlando* (p. Xii). New Haven, CT: Yale University Press.
7. Koenig, D. (2014). *Realityland: True-Life Adventures at Walt Disney World*, "The Undercover Expansion." Irvine, CA: Bonaventure Press.
8. Florida Industrial and Phosphate Research Institute (2020, October 9). Retrieved November 16, 2020, from https://fipr.floridapoly.edu/.
9. Florida Industrial and Phosphate Research Institute (2020, October 9).
10. Foglesong, R. E. (2003).
11. Foglesong, R. E. (2003).
12. Foster, R. (1992).
13. Koenig, D. (2014).
14. Foster, R. (1992).
15. Foster, R. (1992).
16. Foster, R. (1992).
17. Foster, R. (1992).
18. Foster, R. (1992).
19. Foster, R. (1992).
20. Foster, R. (1992).
21. Foster, R. (1992).
22. Foster, R. (1992).
23. Foglesong, R. E. (2003).
24. Foster, R. (1992).
25. Foster, R. (1992).
26. Foster, R. (1992).
27. Foster, R. (1992).
28. Foglesong, R. E. (2003).
29. Foster, R. (1992).
30. Foster, R. (1992).
31. Foster, R. (1992).
32. Foster, R. (1992).
33. Foster, R. (1992).
34. Foster, R. (1992).
35. Foster, R. (1992).
36. Foster, R. (1992).
37. Walt Disney Archives (n.d.). *D23: The Official Disney Fan Club*, "Disney Legends: Joe Fowler." Retrieved November 16, 2020, from https://d23.com/walt-disney-legend/joe-fowler/.
38. Foster, R. (1992).
39. Foster, R. (1992).

40. Foster, R. (1992).

41. Emerson, C., Cockerell, L., & Solt, J. (2010). *Project Future: The Inside Story Behind the Creation of Disney World.* Charleston, SC: Ayefour Publishing.

42. Foster, R. (1992).

43. Foster, R. (1992).

44. Foster, R. (1992).

Chapter Six

1. Foster, R. (1992). *The Founding of a Kingdom.* Unpublished manuscript, RCID Walt Disney World Files, Robert Foster, University of Central Florida, Orlando.

2. Zehnder, L. E. (1975). *Florida's Disney World: Promises and Problems,* "The Year of Transition." Tallahassee, FL: Peninsular Pub.

3. Zehnder, L. E. (1975).

4. Zehnder, L. E. (1975).

5. Zehnder, L. E. (1975).

6. Zehnder, L. E. (1975).

7. Foster, R. (1992).

8. Foster, R. (1992).

9. Foglesong, R. E. (2003). *Married to the Mouse: Walt Disney World and Orlando* (p. Xii). New Haven, CT: Yale University Press.

10. Fjellman, S. (1992). *Vinyl Leaves: Walt Disney World and America.* Boulder, CO: Westview Press.

11. Dickinson, J. W. (2006, July 9). *Orlando Sentinel,* "Big Mystery Simmered In Summertime of '65."

12. Goldberg, A. H. (2016). *The Disney Story: Chronicling the Man, the Mouse, and the Parks.* Philadelphia, PA: Quaker Scribe Publishing.

13. Foglesong, R. E. (2003).

14. Foglesong, R. E. (2003).

15. Goldberg, A. H. (2016).

16. Foster, R. (1992).

17. Vagnini, S. (2016, September 28). *D23: The Official Disney Fan Club,* "How Walt Disney World Found Its Home in Florida." Retrieved November 16, 2020, from https://d23.com/we-say-its-disney/.

18. Lebowitz, L. (1993, March 31). *Orlando Sentinel,* "Cattleman, Politician Oren Brown, 85, Dies."

19. Dickinson, J. W. (2006, July 9).

20. Foster, R. (1992).

21. Foster, R. (1992).

22. Foster, R. (1992).

23. Foster, R. (1992).

24. Foster, R. (1992).

25. Zehnder, L. E. (1975).
26. Foster, R. (1992).
27. ProgressCityPublicTV (2013, November 30). "Disney World Press Conference (1965)." Retrieved November 16, 2020, from https://www.youtube.com/watch?v=TmJPSjhveSA.
28. ProgressCityPublicTV (2013, November 30).
29. Vagnini, S. (2016, September 28).
30. Foster, R. (1992).
31. Foster, R. (1992).
32. Goldberg, A. H. (2016). *The Disney Story: Chronicling the Man, the Mouse, and the Parks*. Philadelphia, PA: Quaker Scribe Publishing.

Chapter Seven

1. Koenig, D. (2014). *Realityland: True-Life Adventures at Walt Disney World*, "The Undercover Expansion." Irvine, CA: Bonaventure Press.
2. Sklar, M. (1967, September 21). *Walt Disney World: Background and Philosophy*. Burbank, CA.
3. Zehnder, L. E. (1975). *Florida's Disney World: Promises and Problems*, "The Year of Transition." Tallahassee, FL: Peninsular Pub.
4. Zehnder, L. E. (1975).
5. Foglesong, R. E. (2003). *Married to the Mouse: Walt Disney World and Orlando* (p. Xii). New Haven, CT: Yale University Press.
6. Foster, R. (1992). *The Founding of a Kingdom*. Unpublished manuscript, RCID Walt Disney World Files, Robert Foster, University of Central Florida, Orlando.
7. Foster, R. (1992).
8. Foster, R. (1992).
9. Foster, R. (1992).
10. Foster, R. (1992).
11. Foster, R. (1992).
12. Buntin, J. (2018, April). *Governing.com*, "Outside Disneyland, a Reminder for Governments to Be Careful What They Wish for." Retrieved from https://www.governing.com/topics/mgmt/gov-disneyland-anaheim-incentives.html.
13. Foster, R. (1992).
14. Foster, R. (1992).
15. Foster, R. (1992).
16. Foster, R. (1992).
17. Foster, R. (1992).
18. Foster, R. (1992).
19. Foster, R. (1992).
20. Foster, R. (1992).

21. TheOriginalEpcot (2013, March 5). "Walt Disney's original E.P.C.O.T film (1966) SD FULL VERSION." Retrieved November 16, 2020, from https://www.youtube.com/watch?v=_GOYu05GknY.
22. TheOriginalEpcot (2013, March 5).
23. TheOriginalEpcot (2013, March 5).
24. Goldberg, A. H. (2016). *The Disney Story: Chronicling the Man, the Mouse, and the Parks*. Philadelphia, PA: Quaker Scribe Publishing.
25. Goldberg, A. H. (2016).
26. Zehnder, L. E. (1975).
27. Foster, R. (1992).
28. Foster, R. (1992).
29. Foster, R. (1992).
30. Foster, R. (1992).
31. Foster, R. (1992).
32. Foglesong, R. E. (2003).
33. Foglesong, R. E. (2003).
34. Zehnder, L. E. (1975).
35. Goldberg, A. H. (2016).
36. Zehnder, L. E. (1975).
37. Lawrence, D. (1967, April 12). *Orlando Sentinel*, p. 9, "House Chief Sees No Blocks For Proposals."
38. Zehnder, L. E. (1975).
39. Koenig, D. (2014).
40. Foster, R. (1992).
41. Foglesong, R. E. (2003).
42. Foglesong, R. E. (2003).
43. Foglesong, R. E. (2003).
44. Foglesong, R. E. (2003).
45. Foglesong, R. E. (2003).
46. Foglesong, R. E. (2003).

Chapter Eight

1. Fickley-Baker, J. (2012, May 30). *Disney Parks Blog*, "Today in Disney History: Disney Broke Ground On Walt Disney World Resort 45 Years Ago." Retrieved November 16, 2020, from https://disneyparks.disney.go.com/blog/2012/05/today-in-disney-history-disney-broke-ground-on-walt-disney-world-resort-45-years-ago/.
2. Zehnder, L. E. (1975). *Florida's Disney World: Promises and Problems*, "The Year of Transition." Tallahassee, FL: Peninsular Pub.
3. Vagnini, S. (2016, September 29). *D23: The Official Disney Fan Club*, "King of the World: What it Was Like to Live at Walt Disney World." Retrieved November 16, 2020, from https://d23.com/king-of-the-world-what-it-was-

like-to-live-at-walt-disney-world.

4. Vagnini, S. (2016, September 29).
5. Ghez, D. (2011). *Joe & Carl: Two Men Who Built the World*; Emerson, C. D. (2011, January 6). *Four Decades of Magic: Celebrating the First Forty Years of Disney World*. Pike Road, AL: Ayefour Publishing.
6. Pedicini, S. (2015, May 22). *Orlando Sentinel*, "Walt Disney World's city residents help keep the resort running."
7. Pedicini, S. (2015, May 22).
8. Mirarchi, C. (2016, August 30). *Disney Information Station*, "Roy O. Disney's Home Away From Home." Retrieved November 16, 2020, from https://www.wdwinfo.com/history/roy-o-disneys-home-away-from-home/.
9. Office of Program Policy Analysis and Government Accountability (2004). *Report No. 04-81*, "Central Florida's Reedy Creek Improvement District Has Wide-Ranging Authority."
10. Office of Program Policy Analysis and Government Accountability (2004).
11. RCID Information (2020, November 1). [E-mail to 1059012751 807522494 E. Washington].
12. Office of Program Policy Analysis and Government Accountability (2004).
13. Foster, R. (1992). *The Founding of a Kingdom*. Unpublished manuscript, RCID Walt Disney World Files, Robert Foster, University of Central Florida, Orlando.
14. Hill, J. (1987, January 12). *Orlando Sentinel*, "It Is Indeed a Small World After All Residents of Bay Lake and Lake Buena Vista."
15. Mirarchi, C. (2016, August 30).
16. Zehnder, L. E. (1975).
17. Zehnder, L. E. (1975).
18. Walt Disney Archives (n.d.). *D23: The Official Disney Fan Club*, "Disney Legends: Joe Potter." Retrieved November 16, 2020, from https://d23.com/walt-disney-legend/joe-potter/.
19. Walt Disney Archives (n.d.). *D23: The Official Disney Fan Club*, "Disney Legends: Joe Potter."
20. Walt Disney Archives (n.d.). *D23: The Official Disney Fan Club*, "Disney Legends: Joe Fowler." Retrieved November 16, 2020, from https://d23.com/walt-disney-legend/joe-fowler/.
21. Walt Disney Archives (n.d.). *D23: The Official Disney Fan Club*, "Disney Legends: Joe Fowler."
22. Ghez, D. and Pierce, T. J. (2014). *Walt's People: Talking Disney with the Artists Who Knew Him* (pp. 362–364). United States: Theme Park Press.
23. Pierce, T. J. (2016). *Three Years in Wonderland: The Disney brothers, C. V. Wood, and the Making of the Great American Theme Park*. Jackson: University Press of Mississippi.
24. Pierce, T. J. (2016).

25. Ghez, D. (2011); Emerson, C. D. (2011, January 6).
26. Walt Disney Archives (n.d.). *D23: The Official Disney Fan Club,* "Disney Legends: Donn Tatum." Retrieved November 16, 2020, from https://d23.com/walt-disney-legend/donn-tatum/.
27. Walt Disney Archives (n.d.). *D23: The Official Disney Fan Club,* "Disney Legends: Card Walker." Retrieved November 16, 2020, from https://d23.com/walt-disney-legend/card-walker/.
28. Walt Disney Archives (n.d.). *D23: The Official Disney Fan Club,* "Disney Legends: Dick Nunis." Retrieved November 16, 2020, from https://d23.com/walt-disney-legend/dick-nunis/.
29. Walt Disney Archives (n.d.). *D23: The Official Disney Fan Club,* "Disney Legends: Dick Nunis."
30. Zehnder, L. E. (1975).
31. Fjellman, S. (1992). *Vinyl Leaves: Walt Disney World and America.* Boulder, CO: Westview Press.
32. Fjellman, S. (1992).
33. Fjellman, S. (1992).
34. Fjellman, S. (1992).
35. Fjellman, S. (1992).
36. Fjellman, S. (1992).
37. Zehnder, L. E. (1975).
38. Foglesong, R. E. (2003). *Married to the Mouse: Walt Disney World and Orlando* (p. Xii). New Haven, CT: Yale University Press.
39. Koenig, D. (2014). *Realityland: True-Life Adventures at Walt Disney World,* "The Undercover Expansion." Irvine, CA: Bonaventure Press.
40. Koenig, D. (2014).
41. Zehnder, L. E. (1975).
42. McCleary, E. (1971, June–July). *National Wildlife,* "Will 10,000 People Ruin All This?"
43. McCleary, E. (1971, June–July).
44. Walt Disney Productions (1982). *Walt Disney World: The First Decade* (pp. 9–10). Anaheim, CA: Walt Disney Productions.
45. Walt Disney Productions (1982).
46. RCID Information (2020, November 1).
47. Walt Disney Productions (1982).
48. *The Story of Walt Disney World* (1980). Florida (publisher not identified).
49. *The Story of Walt Disney World* (1980).
50. Ghez, D. (2011); Emerson, C. D. (2011, January 6).
51. Zehnder, L. E. (1975).
52. Zehnder, L. E. (1975).
53. Koenig, D. (2014).
54. Koenig, D. (2014).

55. Koenig, D. (2014).
56. Koenig, D. (2014).
57. Koenig, D. (2014).
58. Koenig, D. (2014).
59. Ghez, D. (2011); Emerson, C. D. (2011, January 6).
60. O'Day, T. (2020, January 14). *Disney Parks Blog,* "The Art of Preview Magic." Retrieved November 16, 2020, from https://disneyparks.disney. go.com/blog/2020/01/the-art-of-preview-magic/.
61. Koenig, D. (2014).
62. Zehnder, L. E. (1975).
63. Foglesong, R. E. (2003).
64. Foglesong, R. E. (2003).
65. Whitney, C. E. (Publisher) (1972, June). *Architectural Forum,* "Walt Disney World: No Mere Amusement Park."
66. Mirarchi, C. (2011). Emerson, C. D. (2011, January 6). *Four Decades of Magic: Celebrating the First Forty Years of Disney World.* Pike Road, AL: Ayefour Publishing.
67. Ghez, D. (2011); Emerson, C. D. (2011, January 6).
68. Ghez, D. (2011); Emerson, C. D. (2011, January 6).
69. Ghez, D. (2011); Emerson, C. D. (2011, January 6).
70. Fjellman, S. (1992).
71. *The Story of Walt Disney World* (1980).
72. *The Story of Walt Disney World* (1980).
73. *The Story of Walt Disney World* (1980).
74. *The Story of Walt Disney World* (1980).
75. *The Story of Walt Disney World* (1980).
76. Zehnder, L. E. (1975).
77. Zehnder, L. E. (1975).
78. Walt Disney Productions (1982).
79. Walt Disney Productions (1982).
80. Walt Disney Productions (1982).
81. Ghez, D. (2011); Emerson, C. D. (2011, January 6).
82. Ghez, D. (2011); Emerson, C. D. (2011, January 6).
83. Goldberg, A. H. (2016). *The Disney Story: Chronicling the Man, the Mouse, and the Parks.* Philadelphia, PA: Quaker Scribe Publishing.
84. Goldberg, A. H. (2016).
85. Goldberg, A. H. (2016).
86. Fjellman, S. (1992).
87. Goldberg, A. H. (2016).
88. Goldberg, A. H. (2019). *Meet the Disney Brothers.* Philadelphia, PA: Quaker Scribe Publishing.
89. Goldberg, A. H. (2019).

90. Goldberg, A. H. (2019).
91. Goldberg, A. H. (2016).

Opening Day

1. Goldberg, A. H. (2016). *The Disney Story: Chronicling the Man, the Mouse, and the Parks.* Philadelphia, PA: Quaker Scribe Publishing.
2. Zehnder, L. E. (1975). *Florida's Disney World: Promises and Problems,* "The Year of Transition." Tallahassee, FL: Peninsular Pub.
3. Goldberg, A. H. (2016).
4. Goldberg, A. H. (2016).

ABOUT AARON

Aaron H. Goldberg is an alumnus of the University of Pennsylvania, from which he graduated with a bachelor's and a master's degree in anthropology. He is the author of the best-selling and award-winning books *The Disney Story: Chronicling the Man, the Mouse, and the Parks*; *Meet the Disney Brothers*; and *The Wonders of Walt Disney World*.

Aaron has been featured in stories about Disney on CNN, *Travel + Leisure* magazine, the *Los Angeles Times*, the *Huffington Post*, and *POPSUGAR*. You can visit him on the web at aaronhgoldberg. com or follow him on Twitter at @aaronhgoldberg.

More Great Books by Aaron!

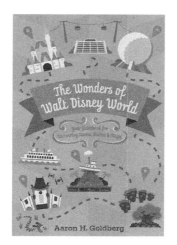

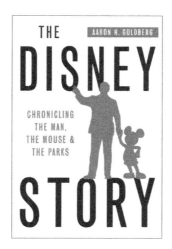

aaronhgoldberg.com